P9-DFV-620

Playing Safe

Playing Safe

Science and the Environment

Jonathon Porritt

Thames & Hudson

For Sarah,
a real scientist

© 2000 Jonathon Porritt

First published in paperback in the United States of America in 2000 by Thames & Hudson Inc., 500 Fifth Avenue, New York, New York 10110

Library of Congress Catalog Card Number 99-66984
ISBN 0-500-28073-8

Printed and bound in Slovenia by Mladinska Knjiga

Contents

Introduction

This book was written over a period of a few months when scientific issues dominated the UK media in an unprecedented way. In the aftermath of the scandal about 'mad cow disease', the British public has been sensitized to similar concerns across a broad range of food, health and environmental issues, from genetically modified food to climate change. This provided a turbulent and unsettling context in which to marshal my ideas about science and the environment, but powerfully confirmed (if confirmation was needed) that the significance of such issues in our lives can only increase.

I should say at the outset that I am not a scientist. I wrestle with the complexities of these issues in much the same way as most MPs, most businesspeople, most journalists and indeed most non-scientific citizens find themselves wrestling with them.

And I wrestle too with my views about science itself and the role of science in our lives. As a 'veteran environmentalist', looking on in despair at the mess we're making of this beautiful planet, I find myself inevitably locating modern science at the very heart of an inherently destructive model of progress, while simultaneously looking to science to provide answers to the otherwise intractable problems we now face. In that respect, I am as ambivalent as the next person, in awe of what science seems to promise, yet fearful of its impact on our lives and deeply critical of the scientific elites who wield such influence in modern society.

Playing Safe is an attempt to rationalize that ambivalence – but not to resolve it one way or another; indeed, I have come to despise equally both the cornucopian fantasies of those who can't think beyond the next technological fix, and the dyspeptic, dystopian fundamentalism of those who scapegoat science and technology as the easiest way of avoiding some of the less palatable truths about human nature.

But my starting premise couldn't be simpler. After decades of ignoring the implications of what we are doing to the Earth, we now know that our current way of life is wholly unsustainable. In evolutionary terms, unsustainability ultimately equals extinction. Sustainability is, therefore, not an option; it is a non-negotiable imperative.

From which flows one simple question: is modern science in a fit state – philosophically, methodologically, politically – to assist us in making that necessary transition from today's unsustainable way of life to a genuinely sustainable future for the whole of humankind?

The postwar model of science that took on the challenges of scarcity and poverty is still broadly admired, even though we may be less inclined to look up to scientists as our 'secular priests' than we once were. In America in particular, the majority of people still instinctively associate science and technology with improvements in their quality of life and personal wealth. But how well adapted is that model to meeting the very different challenge of sustainability?

That's another question that most individual scientists would feel ill-equipped to answer. As specialists, theirs is a tiny slice of the total scientific enterprise, discussed in depth only by fellow specialists. Yet who answers for modern science? Who takes responsibility for the widening gap between their cutting-edge scientific knowledge and the blank incomprehension of the vast majority of people – including those who claim to represent them in Parliament? Who can we hold to account for the erosion of democratic control that this widening gap inevitably entails? How can we harness and manage that super-abundant dynamism – and the technologies that flow from it – rather than find ourselves side-lined as the passive recipients, for good or ill, of the largesse it lays before us?

As we all know, he who pays the piper calls the tune. And the biggest paymasters of science today are the world's multinational companies, for whom the pursuit of sustainability is indisputably less important than the pursuit of profit. Even governments which have theoretically signed up to the 1992 Earth Summit consensus on sustainable development, are still reluctant to shift their not inconsiderable research budgets in the direction of 'science for sustainability'.

Frankly, the signals at the moment are not good. There is an arrogance about modern science that makes regulation by government difficult and true public accountability impossible. Those scientists who retain a vision of science directly serving humankind (not least by securing the Earth's life-support systems on which all else depends) are overshadowed by those who would set caution aside and let modern science rip.

But for how much longer? In contrast to the rather gloomy outlook above, the optimist in me says we're on the brink of a profound transformation of *all* the central institutions in our society, including both politics and science, as we finally internalize the real challenge of sustainability. In some small way, I hope *Playing Safe* will be seen as part of that all-important transformation.

Jonathon Porritt

January 2000

CHAPTER 1

SCIENCE IN THE ENVIRONMENT

In a way that many scientists find quite baffling, they no longer command our unquestioning trust and respect. In both America and Europe, there are very mixed feelings about the role scientists now play in society – and nowhere is this ambivalence more plainly visible than in the field of the environment.

On the one hand, there is deep unease about the wisdom of looking to science as the ultimate arbiter of authority in modern society; understandable anger at the role scientists seem to have played in either tolerating or actively promoting some of the most damaging of today's environmental abuses; constant suspicion of the degree to which science has been commercialized, and has now become the creature of big business (or of governments who are themselves the creatures of big business); and astonishment at the easy ability of so many scientists to remain indifferent to the fact that the planet seems to be disappearing down the evolutionary plughole as they pursue increasingly specialized areas of knowledge of decreasing value to society at large.

On the other hand, there is a rock-solid realization that modern science has brought us startling benefits – and will no doubt continue to do so; that the expert marshalling of solid empirical data is what has actually forced our politicians to start addressing the environmental crisis; that future political and economic programmes can only be justified in terms of exercising the most sophisticated scientific judgment when making complex trade-offs between competing interests; and that there are tens of thousands of individual scientists already personally committed (in both their world view and their practice) to using their knowledge for rather different ends – to create a more sustainable, equitable and compassionate world.

This ambivalence was eloquently elaborated by Bryan Appleyard in his impassioned critique of science, *Understanding the Present: Science and the Soul of Modern Man* (1992):

> Concern for the environment is our age's mechanism for resolving the contradictions inherent in the two opposing aspects of science. Environmentalism is based on scientific insight, and yet it is violently opposed to the effects of most of the more obvious and spectacular achievements of science and technology. It is a way of turning science against itself, of rejecting the progressive ideals of economic growth by using scientific means to expose them as potentially suicidal. It is the single most successful popular solution to the terrible contrast between penicillin and atom bombs, air conditioning and concentration camps.

You can either subscribe to the kind of deeply dyspeptic views espoused by the likes of Edward Goldsmith (editor of the evergreen and still wonderfully instructive *Ecologist* magazine) and Ulrich Beck ('science and technology are running out of control, and everywhere threaten alienation, death and destruction'), or to the resolutely upbeat optimism that still underpins contemporary models of industrial progress and scientific materialism.

Different generations have tended to position themselves at different points on that continuum. People's belief in the benign influence of science was particularly strong in the postwar period, and was rekindled in Britain in the 1960s through Labour Prime Minister Harold Wilson's astute promotion of 'the white heat of technology'. But that kind of blind trust started to erode at the time of the Vietnam War, took a severe knock in the US at the time of the Three Mile Island nuclear accident, and, in the UK at least (for reasons to which we shall return in due course), fell to its nadir around the time of the fiasco caused by the outbreak of bovine spongiform encephalopathy (BSE), or 'mad cow disease' as it was instantly dubbed by the media in the early '90s. Far fewer people now subscribe to the notion of scientific progress with the naïve respect and enthusiasm that was once common. We have learned the hard way that for almost all 'scientific breakthroughs' there is a corresponding downside, with the result that people are much more wary about gung-ho scientific visions of the future.

In an editorial commenting on some of the latest 'breakthroughs' in human genetics in November 1998, the *Daily Mail* tapped into an even deeper layer of unease:

> This uneasiness is not hard to understand. It is not simply the feeling that science is advancing at a pace that leaves most of us in a state of almost total incomprehension. In this century, that feeling has long been familiar. No, it is something older and more basic, something that previous generations would have unhesitatingly and unselfconsciously identified as the fear that scientists are 'playing God'. Though we would welcome the advertised benefits of these breakthroughs, we cannot help suspecting that such work is driven by a blinkered arrogance that will inevitably lead to calamity.

These conflicting currents of public opinion have a particular fascination for me. As a non-scientist, with a couple of average 'O' Levels in Chemistry and Physics, a degree in Modern Languages, and ten years as a teacher of English and Drama, I have had to struggle to keep up with 'the science' of dozens of different single issues out of which the tapestry of contemporary environmentalism is woven. From my very first meeting as a brand new member of the Ecology Party in 1974 (at which all seven of us present were subjected to a technical treatise on the threats to human health caused by the mounting problem of dog faeces on the streets of London!) through to my involvement in the late '90s in The Natural Step (a Swedish initiative to which I shall return in Chapter 7), science has loomed very large in my life as an environmental activist.

The State of the Earth

The discipline of developing what I hope is now a reasonably well-informed scientific approach has made it easier to cope on a personal level with an unstoppable flow of information about the dire state of the Earth. Twenty-five years on from when I first started, things really aren't that much better. Almost all the principal indicators of planetary wellbeing are still heading in the wrong direction; a combination of continuing population growth and rampant materialism ensures that the potential environmental benefits of every incremental efficiency gain are instantly offset by increased consumption; and the far greater levels of public concern and commitment that we see today are cleverly 'managed' by politicians who have now got the hang of environmental rhetoric without taking enough of the difficult decisions on which our prospects of achieving a genuinely sustainable society entirely depend.

On 18 November 1992, just a few months after the Earth Summit in Rio de Janeiro, a document entitled *World Scientists' Warning to Humanity* was released. It was signed by more than sixteen hundred eminent scientists from all over the world, including more than half of all Nobel Laureates in the sciences. Having analysed stresses to the atmosphere, water resources, oceans, soil, forests and living species, they then delivered this warning, which is worth quoting at some length:

> Human beings and the natural world are on a collision course. Human activities inflict harsh and often irreversible damage on the environment and on critical resources. If not checked, many of our current practices put at serious risk the future that we wish for human society and the plant and animal kingdoms, and may so alter the living world that it will be unable to sustain life in the manner that we know. Fundamental changes are urgent if we are to avoid the collision our present course will bring about.
>
> The Earth is finite. Its ability to absorb wastes and destructive effluent is finite. Its ability to provide food and energy is finite. Its ability to provide for growing numbers of people is finite. And we are fast approaching many of the Earth's limits. Current economic practices which damage the environment, in both developed and underdeveloped nations, cannot be continued without the risk that vital global systems will be damaged beyond repair. No more than one or a few decades remain before the chance to avert the threats we now confront will be

lost, and the prospects for humanity immeasurably diminished. We the undersigned, senior members of the world's scientific community, hereby warn all humanity what lies ahead. A great change in our stewardship of the Earth and the life on it is required if vast human misery is to be avoided and our global home on this planet is not to be irretrievably mutilated.

Nothing has changed since then to diminish the gravity of that warning. Yet politicians the world over continue to peddle redundant visions of industrial progress to their consumption-driven electorates, responding to this stark ecological reality by trimming their business-as-usual strategies with a few token environmental flourishes.

In December 1998, the World Wide Fund for Nature brought out its *Living Planet* report with a simple headline: the human species has destroyed more than 30 per cent of the Earth's natural wealth since 1970. With specific reference to three key ecosystems (forests, fresh water and marine), this was the first time anyone had tried to measure the change in the global environment as a whole. Though comparisons are obviously problematic, it was hardly surprising that the commentators' closest point of reference in reporting these data was the extinction of the dinosaurs 65,000,000 years ago.

It is impossible not to feel real pain at the consequences of that 'huge death-wish hanging over the whole so-called civilized world' (as Philip Sherrard, author of *Human Image: World Image*, put it in 1992), in terms of the loss of beauty and mystery, the endless lacerations on the face of the Earth, the suffering of other creatures. Evolutionary biology reassures us, of course, that these are very minor assaults on the fabric of life, barely measurable when set against earlier extinction spasms caused by meteorite impacts or dramatic climate change.

In the presence of that pain, like most environmentalists, I have often given way to sentimental rhetoric about the 'fragility' of the Earth and the delicacy of the web of life. Lynn Margulis, Professor in the Department of Geosciences at the University of Massachusetts, makes short shrift of all such purple prose:

We cannot put an end to nature; we can only pose a threat to ourselves. The notion that we can destroy all life, including bacteria thriving in the water tanks of nuclear power plants or boiling hot vents, is ludicrous. I hear our non-human brethren snickering: 'Got along without you before I met you, gonna get along without you now,' they sing about us in harmony. Most of them, the microbes, the whales, the insects, the seed plants, and the birds, are still singing. The tropical forest trees are humming to themselves, waiting for us to finish our arrogant logging so they can get back to their business of growth as usual. And they will continue their cacophonies and harmonies long after we are gone.

She's right. The science from which she derives such insights is indisputably right – *pace* a few Christian fundamentalists who believe that God just set the whole life thing in motion about ten thousand years ago. But that does little to take away the pain, as Theodore Roszak points out in *The Voice of the Earth* (1992):

A culture that can do so much to damage the planetary fabric that sustains it, and yet continues along its course unimpeded, is mad with the madness of a deadly compulsion that reaches beyond our own kind to all the brute innocence about us. And the loss that comes of that crime falls upon us as much as upon any species of plant or animal we annihilate; for the planet will, of course, endure, perhaps to generate new adventures in life in the aeons to come. But we are being diminished by our destructive insensitivity in ways that cripple our ability to enjoy, grow, create. By becoming so aggressively and masterfully 'human', we lose our essential humanity.

I'm not at all convinced that modern science is of much help when it comes to retrieving 'our essential humanity'. But it is at least true that politicians today are able to call on a much more extensive and robust body of scientific data to help them get to grips with this crisis. It is worth remembering that prior to 1972 (the date of the first United Nations Conference on the Environment and Human Development in

Stockholm), hardly any government had a designated Environment Department, there were few if any statutory bodies like the US Environment Protection Agency or English Nature, research budgets were tiny, and most universities had little interest in the environment as an academic discipline beyond traditional ecology or geography departments.

Our 'capacity' to monitor and analyse the impact of human societies on the Earth's life-support systems has therefore been greatly enhanced. As we'll see, there are still substantial areas of disagreement between scientists on almost all the major controversial issues that keep hitting the media, but no environmentalist today could any longer claim that science establishments around the world are ignoring the ecological crisis.

But why, then, is there such a chronic and ever-widening gap between the uncontested evidence of worsening environmental degradation (let alone that which is still contested) and the wholly inadequate policy response from governments? Why is it that economists (the most arrogant and environmentally ignorant of all academic pseudo-sciences) still hold politicians in thrall, obscuring hard physical reality in a miasma of self-serving, denatured abstractions? Why is it that there's not a single world leader of any stature who uses his or her democratic mandate and authority to make people sit up and understand that this stuff isn't going to go away just because it's a bit uncomfortable?

Do We Trust Our Scientists?

So the gap between the data and the appropriate policy response still widens, even though the world of contemporary environmental policy-making is now permeated through and through with authoritative science of every description. But there's an intriguing paradox at work here: for all that we need and depend on our scientists, technologists, and engineers more than ever before if we are to meet the challenge of sustainability, their current standing in society is at a dangerously low ebb, and the general public seems less and less inclined to put its faith in science in the way it once so readily did.

The UK polling organization MORI regularly tracks public attitudes towards scientists, comparing their standing with that of other professions and occupations. Looking at the latest data, Bob Worcester of MORI points out:

In general, scientists perform reasonably well (but not outstandingly) when compared with other groups on how far the public trust them to tell the truth. In both 1997 and 1999, 63 per cent of the public said they trusted scientists, putting them ahead of the benchmark figure (56 per cent in 1997 and 60 per cent in 1990) of the 'ordinary man/woman in the street', but well behind the most trusted groups, doctors and teachers, and indeed behind professors. By way of contrast, when the Louis Harris polling organization asked an identical question in the USA in 1998, scientists came near the top of the list, trusted to tell the truth by 79 per cent of the American public.

TABLE 1

Q Now I will read out a list of different types of people. For each, would you tell me whether you generally trust them to tell the truth or not?

	April 1997			January 1999		
	Trust %	Not %	Net % +/-	Trust %	Not %	Net % +/-
Doctors	86	10	+76	91	7	+84
Teachers	83	11	+72	89	7	+82
Clergymen/priests	71	20	+51	80	14	+66
Professors	70	12	+58	79	10	+69
Judges	72	19	+53	77	16	+61
Television newsreaders	74	14	+60	74	17	+57
Scientists	63	22	+41	63	27	+36
The police	61	30	+31	61	31	+30
Man/woman in the street	56	28	+28	60	28	+32
Pollsters	55	28	+27	49	35	+14
Civil servants	36	50	-14	47	41	+6
Trade Union officials	27	56	-29	39	47	-8
Business leaders	29	60	-31	28	60	-32
Government ministers	12	80	-68	23	70	-47
Politicians generally	15	78	-63	23	72	-49
Journalists	15	76	-61	15	79	-64

Source: MORI/British Medical Association (1999); *Times* (1997)
Base: c. 1000 (1997); c. 2000 (1999) British adults

An even gloomier picture emerged from the Guardian/ICM poll, carried out in June 1999, where scientists came in lower than the police – but still well ahead, it has to be said, of both politicians and journalists. Additional MORI data has also revealed that this 'general trust' looks very different when the employer or sponsor of the scientists is specifically mentioned.

TABLE 2

Q How much confidence would you have in what each of the following have to say about environmental issues?

	A great deal/a fair amount				
	1995 %	1996 %	1997 %	1998 %	Change 97–98 + / -
Scientists working for environmental groups	82	75	83	75	-8
Scientists working in industry	48	45	47	43	-4
Scientists working for the government	38	32	44	46	+2

	Not very much/not at all				
	1995	1996	1997	1998	Change 97–98
Scientists working for environmental groups	12	20	13	19	+6
Scientists working in industry	45	49	48	50	+2
Scientists working for the goovernment	55	63	50	47	-3

Source: MORI
Base: c. 1000

If we persevere with the analogy of scientists as 'a secular priesthood', then it's clear that the citizens of many European countries have lost their faith. Just as we long ago gave up deferring to bishops or politicians, scientists are now being levelled down in much the same way. Justified or not (and personally I believe much of it to be unjustified), our deep disillusionment about both the effectiveness and the integrity of politicians is having a corrosive effect on the whole body politic – and part of that poison has rubbed off on scientists representing any official government position.

But that alone is not sufficient to explain how scientists have been knocked off their pedestal over the last twenty years or so. Nor is the fact that, being only human, they keep on making mistakes. Great big mistakes, not just basic scientific errors, as Robert Youngson's book, *Scientific Blunders* (1998) lays out for all to enjoy. Scientists are the one group of professionals in society who are always able to make a virtue of error. The scientific method consists in people putting forward new ideas (as hypotheses) and results (as evidence or proof) in the sure knowledge that their peers will do everything in their power to rubbish them if there are any methodological or logical errors. If other scientists replicate the findings, then the hypothesis is judged to be robust – but never definitively correct – and the work moves on from there. Hence Karl Popper's description of the scientific method as one of 'disconfirmation' rather than affirmation. Even so-called 'scientific laws' are in practice no more than working propositions.

It may not be errors of fact that matter to the general public as much as errors of judgment. In his final address as President of the Royal Society in November 1995, fifty years after the first atom bomb destroyed Hiroshima, Sir Michael Attiyah reflected on the consequences of that defining moment for humankind:

> No other single event has so profoundly affected the relationship between science and society. It has cast a very long shadow over the past fifty years. The most immediate effect was to highlight the moral dilemma of scientists in relation to the military application of their discoveries. The technical triumph of the atomic bomb pushed scientists into the military-industrial complex; atomic bombs were a menace, and the scientists were held responsible. This anti-science feeling has grown alarmingly, with environmental worries taking over from nuclear weapons as the driving force.

Science for Sale

Those suspicions are stronger today than they've ever been, and with good reason, given that such a huge percentage of scientists are now paid by private or public sector employers who have little interest in open scientific debate. Official government secrecy, commercial confidentiality, and the ever-present threat of funding being withdrawn, are quite sufficient to button the lips of all but the most courageous.

This is not a new phenomenon. At several points in *Silent Spring*, published in 1962, Rachel Carson comments on the complicity of so many of the government scientists she came into contact with when researching the impact of pesticides on the environment and human health. She sympathized with their dilemma, but had little respect for what she saw as the dereliction of their duty as *scientists*, however dutiful they were as government officials. In private correspondence, she often quoted Abraham Lincoln: 'To sin by silence when they should protest makes cowards of men.'

One can only surmise that Rachel Carson would be distraught at what is happening today, when not just cowardice but 'science for sale' has become a familiar phenomenon (as will be explored in more detail in Chapter 5), and when the stranglehold of large companies has become a great deal tighter than it was when Carson was writing in the early 1960s.

Many leading scientists, especially those who have taken it upon themselves to 'popularize' complex issues, simply refuse to acknowledge either the extent or the significance of this phenomenon of co-option. Steve Jones, an eminent British geneticist and articulate defender of the integrity and benefits to society of modern science, is fond of using a number of reassuring clichés to set people's minds at rest. One of these is 'money doesn't smell', by which he means that the source of any grant or research budget doesn't really matter, as the inherent resilience and integrity of the scientific method will act as a sure and constant bulwark against any nefarious influence.

This is a fairly standard refrain. But Steve Jones and his colleagues should take time out to skim through a devastating critique of the US chemical industry, *Toxic Deception: How the Chemical Industry Manipulates Science, Bends the Law and Endangers Your Health* by Dan Fagin and Marianne Lavelle. Looking in detail at just four of the most commonly used chemicals in America, the authors reviewed 161 studies of those chemicals on file at the National Library of Medicine. Of the 43 industry-funded studies, only 6 came out with any unfavourable findings. Of the 118 studies conducted by non-industry researchers, 71 were unfavourable. It's hard not to detect the reek of money around such findings – and it's worth bearing in mind that of the seventeen hundred or so scientists researching herbicides in the US, 90 percent are employed by chemical companies.

The report goes on to document in detail ways in which the chemical companies have misled the Environmental Protection Agency, acted in 'bad faith', distorted evidence and done everything in their power to keep four very profitable chemicals on the market in a way that would have impressed even the tobacco industry. Commenting on those findings, Charles Lewis, Executive Director of The Center for Public Integrity, trenchantly concluded:

> Simply put, the chemical industry has overpowered the nation's system of safeguarding the public health. The federal agencies that are supposed to be the public's watchdogs have been de-fanged by the industry's pressure tactics, which include junkets and job offers to government regulators, major contributions to politicians, scorched-earth courtroom strategies, and misleading multi-million-dollar advertising and public relations campaigns.

The details of this kind of exposé are not necessarily understood by the general public, but the fact that this skulduggery goes on all the time certainly is. Which is why every time a Steve Jones, or Lewis Wolpert (a former Chairman of the UK's Committee on the Public Understanding of Science) pontificates about science being 'value-free' (on the grounds that science only acquires ethical content when it is applied), many people just fall about laughing. As is now widely recognized, science is 'socially constructed' by all sorts of rules, peer-group pressures, values and expectations.

The persistence of the 'value-free science myth' has a pernicious influence on many aspects of policy-making in this area. If governments really want people to have confidence in the regulatory structures that preside over controversial issues like the use of hormones in raising cattle or genetically modified food, then it would be sensible not to stuff the relevant committees with 'experts' who have transparently vested interests in seeing hormone beef or genetically modified foods prosper. Yet their presence on those committees is often justified on the grounds that they will treat all issues coming before them in a wholly dispassionate and 'value-free' way. Those who point out the obvious absurdity in these arrangements are themselves dismissed as politically motivated, anti-science and 'biased'.

For policy-makers today, simply falling back on the 'tried and tested' value of the conventional scientific method is no longer enough, as is tellingly pointed out by Professor Tim O'Riordan in the latest edition of his authoritative, *Environmental Science for Environmental Management* (1999).

> Science is value-laden, as are the scientists who practise their trade. That is to be expected, though it is not always recognized. More important is the belief that the practice of science may reinforce a non-sustainable economic and social culture. Because we do not know where the margins of sustainability are, the scientific approach may provide a justification for pushing the alteration of the planet beyond the limits of its tolerance. Even by playing safe, the scientific approach may, quite unintentionally, create a sense of false security over the freedom we have to play with the Earth. The critique therefore is directed at the role and self-awareness of science in a world that is grappling for the first time with seeking to restrain human aspiration.

No one would deny that there's a big job to be done retrieving the credibility of science. Apart from the media (who can always make sensational copy out of it), nobody benefits from a climate of automatic, unthinking cynicism and mistrust – least of all those who depend on good science for good decisions. Yet the irony of entrusting this job to scientists who seem to feel only contempt for non-scientists is more than a little striking. It really doesn't help if leading scientists constantly resort to the accusation that those who have different opinions from them are 'ignorant' or 'emotional', or even 'hysterical' – a word that has been much bandied around by scientists in the debate about GM food. There's such a depth of arrogance there, such a lack of humility and respect for other people, that one can almost feel the gap widening even as they speak.

CHAPTER 2

WHOLES AND PARTS

Critics of the current scientific method have delved deep into the history of science to try and explain why it often seems so out of touch with people's deeper concerns. The principles and practice of what is referred to as 'inductive science' were laid down by Francis Bacon in the early seventeenth century. To many, he remains the 'father of modern science', a bold entrepreneurial character who, as Lord Chancellor of England, had no doubt that the role of science was to master nature for economic benefit.

More recently, critics have begun to ask if the seeds of modern science's overbearing arrogance were not in fact sown by the self-same Francis Bacon, as he set in train a 'scientific revolution' which licensed both the unthinking exploitation of Nature and the cruellest oppression of women. In *The Masculine Birth of Time*, Bacon argued, 'I am come in very truth leading to you Nature with all her children to bind her to your service and make her your slave.' The new method of interrogation was 'in very truth to dissect Nature'. In this way, Nature can then be 'forced out of her natural state and squeezed and moulded'. Frequently describing matter as a 'common harlot', he draws on metaphors of sexual domination and torture (as used in the inquisition of the 'witches' of his time) in showing how an inductive scientific method is the means by which knowledge must be won.

It is of course true that Bacon had a mellower side to him ('Man, the servant and interpreter of Nature . . . for Nature is not conquered save by obedience'), and that he believed passionately in maintaining the links between the humanities, religion and science. In that respect, his shade has been summoned up by many leading scientists as an exemplar of 'unified learning' and of the critical need for interdisciplinary thinking as a precondition for engaging properly with the world.

But the harshness and cruelty of his methods and language lingered on well into the nineteenth century.

Eco-feminists from Carolyn Merchant in the 1970s through to Vandana Shiva in the 1990s have systematically sought to expose some of those dark roots of modern science. The central thrust of their criticism is that modern science is somehow incomplete. The enforced rejection of any emotion, let alone passion; the inculcation in young scientists of a calculating, dispassionate and depersonalized scientific method; the narrow focus on tiny slivers of reality, with little apparent interest in the bigger picture; the obsessional self-deception involved in trying to present science as value-free and wholly objective – all have been interpreted as forms of self-mutilation.

In *Lifting the Veil: the Feminine Face of Science* (1997) Linda Jean Shepherd explores five vital qualities that she feels male-dominated scientific establishments continue to miss out on: feeling, nurturing, receptivity, cooperation and intuition – 'all are based on interdependence, a keen awareness of relationship to the other and to the whole'. Is it not possible, as she and many others have suggested, that modern science is so doggedly intent on pursuing 'the masculine path of logic and analysis based on separating and compartmentalizing' that it has lost the art of seeing the whole, of intuiting and constantly acknowledging an inherent interconnectedness between everything?

Since the now commonplace accusation of 'reductionism' has proved to be such a wonderfully red rag to the defenders of modern science, it may be helpful to enter a caveat at the outset: there's nothing wrong with reducing wholes to their constituent parts in order to understand them better. Scientific enquiry demands nothing less, and time after time huge leaps forward in understanding have been achieved in exactly that manner. In his extraordinary book, *Consilience* (1999), E.O. Wilson provides many insights into the benefits of what might be described as 'intelligently applied reductionism':

> Scientists as a rule do not discover in order to know, but rather, as the philosopher Alfred North Whitehead observed, they know in order to discover. They learn what they need to know, often remaining poorly

informed about the rest of the world, including most of science for that matter, in order to move speedily to some part of the frontier of science where discoveries are made. There they spread out like foragers on a picket line, each alone or in small groups probing a carefully-chosen, narrow sector. They are fellow prospectors, pressing deeper into an abstractive world, content most of the time to pick up an occasional nugget, but dreaming of the mother lode. They come to work each day thinking sub-consciously, 'it's there, I'm close, this could be the day.'

The problem resides in the seemingly inevitable tendency in contemporary science to focus in so closely on each individual part that its relationships with other parts, and with the whole of which they are all parts, become invisible. What we end up with, as Canadian geneticist and environmentalist David Suzuki puts it, is 'a fractured mosaic of disconnected bits and pieces, whose parts will never add up to a coherent narrative.' In *The Sacred Balance* (1998) he draws out some of the implications of 'fracturing' reality in this way:

Over time it has become clear that at every level the effort to know the whole from the parts is doomed. At the most elementary level of matter, physicists examining parts of atoms early in this century created a solar-system-like model with discrete protons and neutrons at the centre analogous to the sun, and electrons orbiting the nucleus like the planets. Quantum mechanics destroyed this comforting model by replacing it with an atomic image whose components could only be predicted statistically. That is, the position of a particle could not be defined with absolute certainty, but only by statistical probability. If there is no absolute certainty at the most elementary level, then the notion that the entire universe is understandable and predictable from its components becomes absurd.

That may sound like some philosophical nicety, of little direct relevance to the cut-and-thrust of science in the marketplace today. But more often than not, 'single issue controversies' can be tracked back to this kind of philosophical divide. In Chapter 6, for example, we will discover how the principal concerns of the critics of genetic engineering go to the very heart of the debate about wholes and parts. Is it really wise, they are asking, to treat the genome of any organism as a more or less arbitrary aggregation of stand-alone genes, each exclusively responsible for a discrete aspect of that organism's development or behaviour? In her highly controversial book, *Genetic Engineering: Dream or Nightmare?* (1997), Mae-Wan Ho illuminates the contrast between the prevailing mindset of geneticists and the actual physical reality of how genes work:

> Genetic engineers basically believe that manipulating genes has the potential to solve all major problems of the world, for genes determine the characters of organisms. So by manipulating the appropriate genes, one can engineer organisms to fulfil all our needs. That can only be true if genes determine the characters of organisms in an uncomplicated way, so that, by identifying a gene, one can predict a desirable or undesirable trait; by changing the gene, one changes the trait; by transferring the gene, one transfers the corresponding trait, once and for all. In other words, genetic engineering biotechnology only makes sense if one believes in genetic determinism. Let me highlight the mismatch between mindset and reality below:

Genetic Engineering Mindset	*Reality of Scientific Findings*
1 Genes determine characters in linear causal chain; one gene gives one function.	Genes function in complex network; causation is multi-dimensional, non-linear and circular.
2 Genes and genomes are not subject to environmental influence.	Genes and genomes are subject to feedback regulation.
3 Genes and genomes are stable and unchanging.	Genes and genomes are dynamic and fluid, can change directly in response to the environment and give 'adaptive' mutations to order.
4 Genes stay where they are put.	Genes jump horizontally between unrelated species and recombine.

Yet billions of dollars are now backing 'magic-bullet', single-gene 'solutions' that are conceptualized, developed, tested, sold and hyped against a scientifically flawed and corrupted backdrop. In that respect, genetic engineering is the linear inheritor of the same control fantasies that Francis Bacon so powerfully stood for. Lord Habgood, the former Archbishop of York, has questioned the wisdom of 'genetic determinism' of this kind, where robust claims have been made about single genes determining aspects of complex social behaviour such as aggression, alcoholism or homosexuality.

> Scientific talk about genes for this or that can be very seductive. But genetic determinism makes no sense in creatures as complex, as open to our environment, and as dependent on social interaction as human beings have always known themselves to be. Unless its limitations are made clear, its tendency in the long run is to undermine moral responsibility and our sense of independent personhood.

The Assumption of Separateness

We might just about be able to cope with 'the profound philosophical error of reductionism' were it not compounded by an even graver error: the perverse and incredibly persistent assumption that the human species is a species that stands apart from the rest of nature. As Fritz Schumacher put it in *Small is Beautiful* (1974):

> Modern man does not experience himself as a part of nature, but as an outside force to dominate and conquer it. He even talks of a 'battle' with nature, forgetting that, if he won the battle, he would find himself on the losing side.

For a whole host of different reasons (cultural, religious and political), western science by the eighteenth century was possessed by what Willis Harman has called 'an ontological assumption of separateness' – the separateness of the observer from that which is being observed, of parts from the whole of which they are parts, of individual organisms/genes from their surrounding environment, of humankind from the rest of nature, of mind from matter, of science from religion.

Historically, the 'assumption of separateness' has worked like a psychic toxin in the system, undermining our ability properly to understand our own part in creation, obscuring the incontrovertible empirical reality that as physical entities we humans are, like all organisms, no more and no less interconnected parts of the natural world. It is this poison that feeds the arrogance that allows us to set about the destruction of the natural world as if we were not simultaneously setting about our own destruction.

One of the most compelling accounts of the inseparability of humankind and the rest of life on Earth can be found in David Suzuki's book, *The Sacred Balance: Rediscovering our Place in Nature*, mentioned before. Adopting an elemental style of analysis (by reference back to the physical composition of the air we breathe, the water we drink, the soil in which we grow our food, and the raw materials we use to drive our economies), he illuminates connectedness as the single most important reality in our lives. Check out the argon story below:

The eminent Harvard astronomer, Harlow Shapley, pointed out that while 99 per cent of the air we breathe is highly active oxygen and mildly reactive nitrogen, about 1 per cent is made up of argon, an inert gas. Because it is inert, it is breathed in and out without becoming part of our bodies or entering into metabolic transformations. Shapley calculated that each breath contains about 30,000,000,000,000,000,000 atoms of argon. Suppose you exhale a single breath and follow those argon atoms. Within minutes, they will have diffused in the air far beyond the spot where they were released. After a year, those argon atoms have been mixed up in the atmosphere and spread around the planet in such a way that each breath you take includes at least 15 atoms of argon released in that one breath a year earlier! According to Shapley:
'Your next breath will contain more than 400,000 of the argon atoms that Ghandi breathed in his long life. Argon atoms are here from conversations at the Last Supper, from the arguments of diplomats at Yalta, and from the recitations of the Classic poets. We have argon from

the sighs and pledges of ancient lovers, from the battlecries at Waterloo, even from last year's argonic output by the writer of these lines, who personally has had more than 300,000,000 breathing experiences.'

Arrogant industrialists and politicians have clearly had good cause to set this kind of biophysical reality to one side in the modern pursuit of wealth. But it's hard to understand how such a patently absurd delusion has endured for so long. Philosophers and religious leaders have done little to expose it, let alone generation after generation of scientists. Even those latter-day defenders of the environment (the non-governmental organizations like Friends of the Earth and Greenpeace) may themselves have played some unwitting part in that process, allowing themselves to be seduced by the hard-edged logic of reductionist methodologies.

Robin Grove-White, a former Director of the Council for the Protection of Rural England, and now Director of the Centre for the Study of Environmental Change at Lancaster University, has closely examined the different ways in which today's 'environmental problematique' has been framed by different players – government, NGOs, businesses and so on. He points out that, for wholly understandable reasons, NGOs found themselves drawn ('gravitationally, as it were') to organize themselves in ways that matched the compartmentalized, reductionist structures that the government had adopted when environmental issues first gained their public profile: energy, agriculture, land use and planning, transport, all in their separate boxes. To be effective, NGOs adopted the thought patterns of those whose thoughts they sought to change.

Grove-White's elegantly and closely argued conclusion in *The Political Quarterly* (1997) is a sobering one for environmental NGOs:

Our collective vested interest in prevailing social arrangements – including the culturally dominant *ontology* based on the scientific world view – is deeply embedded and desperately difficult to change. Many of the formulations of even those most committed to 'saving the planet' have embodied a tendency to reproduce, rather than to progress beyond, the particular man-nature divide which has characterized intellectual orthodoxy over much of the past 300 years.

This certainly strikes a personal chord with me. When I became Director of Friends of the Earth in 1984, after ten years in the Ecology/Green Party, I was amazed at the low regard in which FoE was held by scientists. (The irony for me was that Friends of the Earth had been one of the most authoritative sources of scientific information for the Green Party!) This was a huge problem for an organization that had two principal targets: the media and politicians. The truth was that it hadn't much mattered to FoE during the first 15 years of its history whether it 'got the science right' on every occasion; at a time when very few people knew anything about environmental impacts, a little knowledge went a long way in firing up people's anger, indignation or compassion. The gap that had to be filled in those early days was at least as much about emotion and imagination as about rigorous scientific argumentation.

Come the mid-1980s, however, things were changing rapidly. FoE, Greenpeace, WWF and many others had done a good job narrowing the 'caring gap', and being seen to get things right scientifically, and to care about getting things right, was becoming much more important. Painfully but systematically, we therefore increased the amount of money spent on research, using more independent scientific experts, taking on more ambitious projects on issues like acid rain, nuclear power, pesticides and rainforest destruction.

By and large, it worked well. 'Respectable radicalism' became our watchword. FoE's reputation as a scientifically reliable and reputable organization grew throughout the 1980s, and it's still a cherished part of its public image.

But something happened in the process. Fewer risks were taken; intuition and passion became questionable attributes; instead of 'loving nature', even Friends of the Earth began to dissect nature; connections with 'weird and wacky' organizations were frowned on, and anything too overtly spiritual withered on our new reductionist vine. In the pursuit of scientific credibility, Friends of the Earth temporarily lost its soul. Only in retrospect did I come to realize that I too, like so many others, had been sucked in and seduced by the dominant model of science.

It seems all but impossible to celebrate the extraordinary benefits that science has brought humankind (and will undoubtedly continue to do so) without signing up to the dominant world view (aggressive, exploitative, reductionist, arrogant and prejudicial to much that I hold dear about our human potential) which serves as the philosophical bedrock for modern science. The sheer scale of the sustainability challenge demands so much more of science than scientists seem prepared to offer that many environmentalists find themselves falling back (albeit reluctantly) on very different aspects of the human genius – to find meaning and purpose beyond the confines of inductive science in spiritual or religious quests.

When science fails them, or is perceived to fail them, people fall back on their basic values. I find myself at one here with Paul Ehrlich in the views that he expressed in his book *The Machinery of Nature* (1986):

> I'm convinced that a quasi-religious movement, one concerned with the need to change the values that now govern much of human activity, is essential to the persistence of our civilization. But agreeing that science, even the science of ecology, cannot answer all questions – that there are 'other ways of knowing' – does not diminish the absolutely critical role that good science must play if our over-extended civilization is to save itself.

But 'good science' (or 'sound science') remains as elusive a concept as ever. It is used by most politicians and industry scientists in a clinical, minimalist way to convey the importance of methodological rigour, analytical accuracy, sound interpretative judgment, with everything subject to the scrutiny of other scientists through proper 'peer review'. There's nothing wrong with such an approach, in a tautological sort of way, but it doesn't really tell us much about the manner in which science is practised.

The Frankenstein Syndrome

Most radical critiques of modern science are generously peppered with admonitions for it to be 'more like this' and 'less like that', six of which I shall be exploring over the remaining chapters: that science should be more precautionary; more participative; less arrogant; less compromised by its paymasters; more compassionate; and more holistic. And the unspoken implication behind all of that is that 'good science' should be much more explicitly and purposefully geared to improving the lot of humankind.

But in discussing these matters with scientists themselves, one encounters an extraordinary range of responses, from contempt and denial to outright incomprehension. It's so much easier to remain embunkered in the value-free, uncomplicatedly rational world that reductionist science offers – however spuriously – than it is to venture out into the contested territory of 'holistic science' or 'civic science' or 'precautionary science'. Upholders of the scientific faith shudder at the implications of having to mix it with such irredeemably subjective and impure elements.

To give but one example, mainstream scientists' disbelief and deep anger at the way public opinion has turned against genetically modified (GM) food has been a revelation in itself. Such deep-seated 'irrationalism' in people seems to them to threaten the very foundations of modern science. Their outraged indignation at anyone daring to brand GM foods as 'Frankenstein foods' would be funny indeed were it not so revealing of the profound insecurity they must feel.

The headline of the *Daily Mirror* on 16 February 1999 read: 'THE PRIME MONSTER: Fury as Blair Says 'I Eat Frankenstein Food and It's Safe', with a photofit of the Prime Minister made up to look like Frankenstein's monster! This made me wonder, not for the first time, how many people have actually read Mary Shelley's powerful novel, let alone understood the true purpose that lies behind it. Her model for Victor Frankenstein (who is of course the creator of the monster, not the monster itself) was her own husband, Percy Shelley. He was an outright enthusiast for the science of the day, utterly convinced of its benign power to dispel superstition and overcome ignorance. The words she puts in Victor Frankenstein's mouth (as he set out to create a race of superior beings) could be uttered today by any one of the scientists racing to clone human beings: 'I will pioneer a new way, explore unknown powers, and unfold to the world the deepest mysteries of creation.'

As many critics have pointed out, it's extraordinary that this nineteen-year-old woman should have so powerfully captured the vicarious thrill of what was an essentially male scientific quest. Her subtitle, *The Modern Prometheus* (influenced no doubt by her husband's work on his poem *Prometheus Unbound*) reveals her true intent: to signal her alarm at the recklessness of those who get carried away with the intoxication of their own genius. All else is sacrificed – marriage, home, honour, family – in the pursuit of fame.

However much scientists may hate it, the sensational branding of GM foods as Frankenstein foods was therefore a stroke of instinctive tabloid genius. In *The Memoirs of Elizabeth Frankenstein* (1998) Ted Roszak (one of the wisest and most inspiring writers on good science) sums up the enduring symbolic powers of Mary Shelley's novel:

The Frankenstein image cannot be sensibly applied to any one scientific achievement; it is a critique of the scientific soul, the spirit in which all science is undertaken. Mary Shelley insisted that where science touches the lives of people, it requires not genius, but moral wisdom. In my experience, that is not a subject scientists care to face; indeed, as exemplars of pure reason, many seem to believe they have no psychology, no hidden motives, no quirks, no kinks at all. But then already in Shelley's time, science had ceased to be a branch of philosophy and was splintering into ever narrower fields of professional expertise where wisdom plays no part in building a career. Her critique of Promethean science has lost none of its relevance. If we fail to see that, it is because most of what she found Frankensteinian about science has become so institutionalized that it passes for normal.

And that's precisely why so many ordinary, sensible, unhysterical people feel so uneasy when they're on the receiving end of scientists' ever more desperate efforts to offer reassurance. They are wonderfully clever people, of that there is little doubt, but wisdom seems to be in frighteningly short supply.

Or is this perception of a lack of wisdom on the part of scientists merely an indication of the lack of knowledge on our own part? It's difficult not to be astounded at the sheer power, scale and reach of scientific thinking. In terms of advances in our understanding of consciousness, natural systems, quantum theory, genetics and so on, we're living in an enormously rich period of human development. Our lives are being transformed all around us, in ways that both dazzle and disorient us, as Andrew Marr highlighted in a stirring editorial in the London *Independent* in February 1999:

> Between the scientific upper class, the latter-day Leonardos trekking into the brain or sketching the universe, and the majority of voters and politicians in all western democracies, there is now a deep comprehension gap. After decades of smugly acknowledging the 'two-cultures' division between science and the rest of human life, suddenly we find ourselves falling straight down the hole. How did this happen? How did we get to the situation where the most important and interesting ideas are utterly outside the experience of the vast majority of educated people?

I don't know the answer to that. But I do know that we are all struggling to make sense of a process of change so rapid that it permits of no breathing-spaces, no time-outs, no moratoria. That breathless, breakneck pace is in itself one of the most significant elements in an all-pervading sense that the world seems to be getting riskier rather than safer.

CHAPTER 3

WEIGHING UP THE RISKS

At one level, it's all somewhat ridiculous. There can be no doubt that for most of us in the West the world is a much less risky place than it was even fifty years ago, let alone in preceding centuries. Just think back to the disease-ridden, excrement-encrusted conditions, with foul air and filthy water, that public health campaigners found themselves battling against little more than a hundred and fifty years ago!

And yet it sometimes feels as if we're just shuttling from one scare to the next, panic-junkies endlessly in search of the next fix of fear. Although I will sound like a government official in saying this, one can't help but be concerned at the deeply irrational way in which issues are arbitrarily picked up in the media, exploited for every last vestige of panic potential, and then forgotten. It's amazing that some form of advanced 'risk fatigue' hasn't yet set in, but in post-BSE Europe, it's just a question of waiting for the next panic attack.

In a highly influential book, *The Risk Society* (1992) German sociologist Ulrich Beck argues that people are increasingly moving away from preoccupations about class and crude measures of material well-being to concerns about risk and safety. This may be no bad thing (in that any such transition depends on first generating a higher standard of living), but what drives the risk experts crazy is the apparent inability of the vast majority of people to sort out any kind of 'logical risk hierarchy'. For instance, in one year the risk of dying from a smoking habit of ten cigarettes a day is 1 in 200, compared to a risk of 1 in 850 of dying from all natural causes, 1 in 3,300 from any kind of violence, 1 in roughly 10,000 from a road accident, 1 in 10,000,000 from exposure to radiation released from a nuclear power station, and 1 in around 1,000,000,000 from contracting New Variant Creuzfeldt-Jakob's Disease (CJD) from eating beef on the bone!

The gap between the public perception of risk and 'expert assessment' of risk is getting wider. Surveys regularly reveal that people put things like nuclear radiation top of their list of risk factors, and constantly underestimate risks from things like smoking. This used to be attributed almost entirely to distortion in the media (the most overestimated causes of death correlate fairly closely with the most widely and sensationally reported media stories involving fatalities), but given the extensive coverage of the dangers of smoking, such an explanation seems improbable.

The emphasis has now shifted to the question of control: those risks which we take voluntarily are scaled down in seriousness compared to the 'involuntary risks' imposed upon us, often against our will. A number of studies have shown that people are willing to accept risks from activities undertaken voluntarily up to one thousand times greater than risks from involuntary activities. And we remain more worried about 'high-risk, low-frequency events' (like the accident at Chernobyl nuclear power station in 1988) than we are about 'high-frequency, low-risk events' (like road accidents).

So here we are in the middle of one of those complex mismatches. Scientists measure and seek to communicate relative risk in terms of statistical probability; members of the general public receive only as much of that 'objective' statistical analysis as fits with their personalized, pre-existing risk framework, which is in turn shaped by a whole host of different factors and actors depending on attitudes to the wider world and people's perceived place in it.

One can therefore sympathize with those who would like to establish the equivalent of a 'Richter scale', in which risks are classified as high, moderate, low or negligible. Sean Paling, a former Professor of Biology at Oxford, suggests such a scale, with a 'better-get-used-to-it' zone at one end (including things with a high statistical probability like contracting cancer), and 'the Bobbit zone' at the other end (named after the man who had his penis cut off by his furious wife) to cover 'one-off events that happen hardly ever.'

However, both consumers and environmentalists would appear to have become increasingly resistant to the so-called 'objectivist approach' involved in all such top-down risk hierarchies. Making technical estimates of risk is widely acknowledged to be extremely tricky, with endless scope for disagreement amongst the experts. What we're talking about now is a much more 'constructivist approach'. This, in short, means scientists getting down off their high horses and mixing with us ordinary folk to try and make better sense of these complex issues. Which is precisely what the UK's Royal Commission on Environmental Pollution (RCEP) was saying in its October 1998 report, with its call both for greater public involvement in risk management and for greater responsibility on the part of the general public in learning to handle more sophisticated risk assessments.

In its own modest way, the RCEP report represents real progress. Back in 1992, the Royal Society set up a high-level Study Group to look at risk, which ended up with the 'risk assessors' (the natural scientists and engineers – all 'objectivists', as it were) totally at odds with the 'risk perceivers' (the social scientists – all 'constructivists'). The constructivists described risk entirely as 'a social construct', as if statistical probability derived from real-life empirical risk measurement counted for nothing, which, of course, upset the objectivists. The constructivists found the objectivists totally out of touch with the day-to-day reality that shaped their work, namely 'that things which are perceived as real will be real in their consequences'.

In 1999 it all looks rather different. David Slater, former Director of Environmental Protection at the Environment Agency, summed it up with characteristic common sense:

> If you just took the view of the social scientists, we might come to
> the conclusion that there was no point in trying to assess what
> the risks are. My thesis is that we have to start from a position of
> 'sound science', of best available technical understanding and analysis
> of the issues we are dealing with, but that this on its own is not enough.
> We must deal with these in the broader canvas of how these issues are
> perceived by the public, whose environment we are here to protect.
> It is vital not just to know what risks to eliminate, but also what
> risks to take.

However, as we saw in Chapter 2, 'sound science' is not the value-free notion some make it out to be. In a fascinating insight into the hidden politics of Whitehall, Robin Grove-White has suggested that from its inception the Department of the Environment was obsessed with 'sound science' (evidence based on unambiguously robust, empirically derived data) in order to fight its corner more effectively against other government departments, particularly the Department of Trade and Industry, the Treasury and the Ministry of Agriculture, Fisheries and Food (MAFF). These departments had become extremely skilful in exploiting scientific uncertainty or ambiguity in order to come down hard on the side of doing nothing. It took the dynamite of objectively derived 'sound science' to breakup the bureaucrats' logjam of inertia and procrastination over new policy.

But as Grove-White and his colleagues at Lancaster University have demonstrated time after time, apparently objective and value-free 'sound science' is often shaped by 'prior social commitments framing the nature and boundaries of the issue under consideration.' The disposal of the Brent Spar oil rig in 1995 provides an excellent example of the limitations of building an entire policy purely on 'sound science' without consideration of any other factors. The 'best bet' scientifically may well have been to dump the Brent Spar installation in a deep trench in the North Atlantic, and the scientists may well have carried out an exemplary technical analysis of the risks (and benefits) involved in different disposal routes. But they ignored (or appeared to ignore) so many other relevant factors – 'precedent issues', transparency of process, lack of wider participation, symbolic impact, implied collusion between regulators and private sector operators, uncertainties in the assessment of potential ecological damage, and so on. In this case, as a result, the technical risk assessment proved wholly inadequate in persuading people that dumping the Brent Spar constituted the most rational way forward. Shell was forced to back down, and after a couple of years in a Norwegian fjord, the Brent Spar was eventually dismantled on shore.

Virtual Risks

The situation gets even more complicated when dealing with what John Adams (whose 1995 book, *Risk*, is one of the most instructive and accessible on the subject) describes as 'virtual risks'. Some of the statistical probabilities so confidently asserted by scientists are in fact nothing but overconfident expressions of uncertainty:

> Whenever scientists disagree, or confess their ignorance, the lay public is confronted by uncertainty. Virtual risks, risks about which scientists do not know much or cannot agree (e.g. BSE or carcinogens), may or may not be imaginary, but they have real consequences – people act upon the meanings that they impose upon uncertainty.

He gives as an example the 1995 contraceptive pill scare in the UK. Based on preliminary evidence, the Committee on the Safety of Medicines issued a warning that the latest generation of oral contraceptives was 'twice as likely to cause blood clots' as the previous generation. Something resembling a national panic ensued, and a large number of women stopped taking the pill, leading to an estimated eight thousand extra abortions and an unknown number of unplanned pregnancies – both of which carry a far higher health risk than staying on the pill. Only subsequently did it emerge that this doubling (which sounds pretty serious) would result in no more than two extra fatalities a year, with the death of 5 in 1,000,000 women on the pill instead of 3 in 1,000,000. As Kenneth Calman, the Government's Chief Medical Officer at the time, admitted, this was hardly the best example of responsible risk management. John Adams again: 'Science has been very effective in reducing uncertainty, but much less effective in managing it. A scientist's "don't know" is the verbal equivalent of a Rorschach ink blot: Some will hear a cheerful, reassuring message, others will listen to the same words and hear the threat of catastrophe.'

In such circumstances, perhaps the best thing to do is to publish all the relevant data, encourage as much constructive and informed public debate as possible, and then leave it to people to make up their own minds. That sounds fine in theory, from the point of view of taking personal responsibility for our own 'risk account', but it by no means lets governments off the hook of meeting their collective responsibility on behalf of those voting them in or out of power today, and also on behalf of future generations.

Exercising that collective responsibility remains highly problematic. If one can't prove causality, for instance, it's mighty difficult, if not impossible, to assess the level of risk involved. As we'll see in the next chapter, the links between a large number of chemicals that mimic the effect of oestrogen and certain impacts on human health are getting stronger all the time. But a definitive cause-and-effect linkage remains elusive, not least because the levels of exposure involved are often infinitesimally small. Plucking a figure out of the air statistically to capture that kind of risk is just bad science; in dozens of similar circumstances today, there would appear to be no credible way of calculating risk meaningfully.

One of the most telling points in Jeremy Rifkin's absorbing book about genetics, *The Biotech Century* (1998), is that there is simply no way of assessing the potential risks involved in releasing genetically modified organisms into the environment. There is no 'predictive ecology' to allow experts to hypothesize about downstream impacts on other species – and there would appear to be very little interest in developing new risk assessment techniques on the part either of government or of the biotech companies. Confirmation of this can be seen in the response of the insurance industry:

> While the public was fed a steady barrage of revised, updated, and reworked regulatory guidelines, giving the appearance of rigorous scientific oversight, the insurance industry quietly let it be known that it would not insure the release of genetically engineered organisms into the environment against the possibility of catastrophic environmental damage because the industry lacks a risk assessment science – a predictive ecology – with which to judge the risk of any given introduction. In short, the insurance industry clearly understands the Kafkaesque implications of a government regime claiming to regulate a technology in the absence of clear scientific knowledge

of how genetically modified organisms interact, once introduced into the environment.

The question of liability for catastrophic environmental losses or impacts on human health remains unresolved, despite the fact that 35 million hectares in the world (an area roughly one and a half times the size of Britain) have already been planted with a variety of genetically modified crops around the world.

The Precautionary Principle

Enter stage left the Precautionary Principle. Described even by its keenest advocates as 'a rather shambolic concept', the Precautionary Principle was introduced from Germany into EU environmental thinking and policy-making in the early 1980s, and has gradually increased in importance in contemporary environmental policy-making.

A working definition of the Precautionary Principle goes something like this: 'The lack of definitive scientific evidence should not be used as a reason for postponing measures to protect the environment or human health where there are threats of serious or irreversible damage to either.' Like sustainable development itself, the Precautionary Principle can therefore be interpreted in all sorts of different ways to suit all sorts of different (and often conflicting) purposes.

Its first major outing came in the European Union's Ministerial Declaration on the Protection of the North Sea back in 1987, in which it was accepted that: 'In order to protect the North Sea from possibly damaging effects of the most dangerous substances, a precautionary approach is necessary which may require action to control inputs of such substances even before a causal link has been established by absolutely clear scientific evidence.' Since then it has been incorporated into the EU's Maastricht Treaty, the 1992 Earth Summit's Rio Declaration, the Framework Convention on Climate Change, the Biodiversity Convention, the EU's Fifth Environmental Action Plan, and so on.

In *Interpreting the Precautionary Principle* (1994) Tim O'Riordan and James Cameron summarized the six core elements that make the Precautionary Principle so special:

1 Preventative anticipation: willingness to take action in advance of definitive scientific proof on the grounds that it's better to pay a little now than a whole lot more later.

2 Allowing some 'breathing space' for the Earth, its resources and life-support systems, essentially as a concession to our ignorance about how these systems work and what their tolerance thresholds might be.

3 Shifting the duty of care (or 'burden of proof') on to those who are proposing changes or new developments.

4 Due concern for future generations and recognition of their interests (if not rights) in what this generation is doing.

5 Accepting responsibility for our 'former ecological debts', so that those who've done the most damage to date should be the most cautious from now on.

6 Proportionality of cost – to ensure that any restraint which a precautionary approach considers necessary is not unduly costly.

Sounds great, doesn't it? But this has become one of the most controversial areas in environmental science today. *The Economist* magazine has referred to the Precautionary Principle as 'the new mantra of the environment movement', claiming that it is being used to stop legitimate new developments and drive up regulatory costs in a way that the evidence simply doesn't justify. In an interesting and combative pamphlet, *Poisonous Dummies: European Risk Regulation after BSE (1999)*, Bill Durodie of the European Science and Environment Forum accuses EU decision-makers of a 'retreat from reason', and a 'paralysing sensitivity to risk' in their application of the precautionary principle. As well as identifying direct economic costs on businesses affected by the precautionary principle, he alludes to a 'far greater social cost which has yet to be taken into account' – by which he means the cost to society from wasted opportunities and new products foregone as a result of innovators having to proceed with greater caution.

By contrast, Greenpeace sees it as the most effective way of combining science and ethics, and promotes the Precautionary Principle as a long overdue corrective to the overconfident style of development that has dominated the global economy for the last fifty years. Even such a noted champion of trade liberalization as Sir Leon Brittan (the former EU Trade Commissioner) defended the EU's use of the Precautionary Principle 'to preserve our existing levels of environmental and social protection', subject only to it being more rigorously defined 'to prevent it from being invoked in an abusive way.'

And that's the problem. Each of the six core elements referred to above is indeed highly contestable! For each, one can develop either a weak or a strong formulation. Weak formulations would simply mean giving a higher weighting to environmental factors in standard cost-benefit calculations, and devising tougher regulations to take account of the kind of uncertainty factors referred to earlier in the chapter. Strong formulations would mean abandoning viable economic activity on the grounds that 'proof of safety' (which is very different from 'no current proof of damage') could not be provided by developers, as well as introducing new measures to provide absolute protection for critical natural habitats and functions.

It isn't just developers who are hostile to the Precautionary Principle. Many scientists have challenged its scientific validity, deeply suspicious of the way in which it appears to threaten the authority of inductive, cause-and-effect-based science, shifting the balance of power between empirical science and other political or social factors.

The real pinch-point for policy-makers in the UK in the late 1990s has been around the whole question of food safety. The reverberations of the BSE scandal are still loud and ever-present, even though (as we shall see in Chapter 6 regarding genetically modified crops) the lessons have not yet been fully internalized. Labour Ministers oscillate uncomfortably between wanting to set tough new standards for consumer protection and not wanting to create an all-encompassing 'nanny state' in which even the remotest risk has to be legislated against.

The beef-on-the-bone story provides a wonderful case study in just how difficult it is to turn the Precautionary Principle into operational practice. In December 1997, UK Agriculture Minister Jack Cunningham banned cuts of beef still on the bone, having been told by his scientific advisors that nervous tissue in the spinal column could theoretically contain the infectious agent responsible for BSE and possibly new variant CJD. Just over a year later, Nick Brown, the new Agriculture Minister, received the same advice. The level of risk, he was told, was almost too small to measure (with 1 chance in 1,000,000,000 of a person dying in a year, you are seventy times more likely to win the jackpot on the National Lottery than you are to die from eating beef on the bone!), but on a 'precautionary basis', the ban was confirmed.

I hadn't eaten beef for years, apart from the occasional prime organic steak from farmers I happen to know. But this decision irritated me so much that I almost started eating beef again in protest. There has to be a point at which individuals, faced with relatively uncomplicated choices (in this case, to buy or not to buy) are allowed to decide for themselves. With so minute a risk, and with what are perceived to be substantial 'benefits' for beef-eaters on the other side of the equation, the element of precaution in this case seems entirely disproportionate.

Commenting on the beef-on-the-bone fiasco in the London *Times*, Mary Ann Sieghart concluded as follows:

> It is time that Ministers got the business of risk into proportion. They should be allowed to intervene only when the size of the risk justifies it, when the rewards do not offset it, and where citizens cannot choose to avoid the risks themselves. Otherwise, they bring the whole regulatory system into disrepute. Politicians are always berating the public for acting neurotically in the face of food or health scares, but they can hardly expect us to be rational – and to trust them – when they are prepared to act hysterically themselves.

After a sufficient period of time was allowed to pass to avoid too much loss of face, the ban was eventually lifted in December 1999.

As it happens, this was the second occasion on which Nick Brown had relied on the Precautionary Principle to make an important decision. In December 1998, he supported an EU proposal to ban the use of four antibiotics widely used as growth-promoters in animal feeds.

MAFF argues that there is as yet no 'hard evidence' of a serious threat to human health from this particular use of antibiotics, but Agriculture and Health Ministers are more and more concerned that traces of antibiotics could be passed on through the food chain, increasing resistance to medicines based on these same antibiotics.

What few people know is that more antibiotics are used in UK farming than in treating sick people. Virtually all our intensively reared pigs and chickens receive antibiotics in their feed in an attempt to control the diseases which are caused by rearing them in that way in the first place, and also to accelerate growth rates. There is almost certainly widespread illegal use as well as approved uses. A House of Lords Inquiry was trenchant in its conclusion: 'Our Inquiry has been an alarming experience. Misuse and overuse of antibiotics are now threatening to undo all their early promise and success in curing disease . . . our report is a blueprint for action. It must start now if we are not to return to the bad old days of incurable diseases.'

The UK Soil Association (which has been spearheading the campaign against the use of antibiotics in animal feeds) welcomed the EU's proposal, but simultaneously pointed out that it left the field open for farmers simply to switch to other, still legal antibiotics. MAFF knows that, but it also knows that the only long-term solution is to put an end, once and for all, first to the regular use of all antibiotics as growth-promoters, and thereafter to the cruel and wholly unnatural intensive rearing systems that necessitate their use. In this case, any consistent exercise of the Precautionary Principle applied to modern farming would require huge changes, most of which would result in consumers paying more for their meat – as we should indeed be doing. But even to discuss such a prospect is a bridge too far for a government department that has never once been ahead of the game in its long and far from honourable history.

CHAPTER 4

TOXIC SHOCKS

The Precautionary Principle is still seen by many UK government officials as an extremely unwelcome and scientifically corrupt interloper. But particularly in the Ministry of Agriculture, Fisheries and Food (MAFF). Of all government departments in the UK, none has proved more resistant to change in the way we juggle risk and responsibility, nor more obstinate in defending its right to turn a scientific blind eye on behalf of UK farmers. Health, nutrition and environmental issues have all been treated with consistent contempt, and the 'first show me the pile of bodies' approach to policy-making is still engrained in every fibre of its corporate culture – the polar opposite of the Precautionary Principle – requiring definitive evidence linking a specific cause with a specific and serious harmful effect before anything is done. This approach reached its apogee in its handling of the BSE crisis, with disastrous consequences for the whole of UK farming.

Looking at MAFF's historical record, one can't help speculating how any good scientist could have continued to work there without recoiling from the grotesque bias (in determining research agendas, for example), endemic secrecy and continuing cover-ups. And it is by no means clear to its critics that MAFF has even now embraced a reform agenda, notwithstanding the change of government in 1997.

There is no clearer example of this than the way in which MAFF and the Department of Health continue to treat farmers affected by the use of organophosphate pesticides (OPs) in sheep dips. These highly toxic chemicals have been mandated by MAFF for many years, and evidence of their damaging impact on a large number of sheep farmers has been steadily accumulating. Symptoms include severe headaches, depression, debilitating lassitude, an inability to concentrate, severe mood swings and all sorts of non-specific aches and pains. Many farmers have talked of just how close they've come to suicide. Some have already taken that tragic step.

To begin with, MAFF officials and Ministers steadfastly denied that there was anything wrong with these farmers, often quite disgracefully implying that they were just idle malingerers. They then denied that this particular syndrome might in any way be linked with the use of OPs. When that fall-back position itself became untenable, officials sought to play down the severity of the symptoms, blaming farmers for not using protective clothing in the way prescribed by manufacturers.

In November 1998, a report from the Royal College of Physicians and Psychiatrists confirmed that farmers were indeed suffering from 'genuine and often very severe symptoms' – and asked GPs and consultants to be 'more sympathetic'! The report then resorted to the usual line pedalled by MAFF ('no firm evidence' of OP poisoning), notwithstanding the fact that MAFF still refuses to commission a proper study to establish the cause of these symptoms. Yet dozens of independent scientists around the world have provided firm evidence linking OPs with similar symptoms.

The reason for MAFF's attitude is evident to all: if a link is accepted, MAFF will have to pay out tens of millions of pounds in compensation to sheep farmers for having compelled them to use substances that for years have been known to pose a severe health risk to humans. By any standards, this is despicable behaviour; and one has to ask, yet again, what it must feel like as a good scientist in MAFF to see natural justice systematically subverted by such an abuse of proper scientific process.

On the broader front, many scientists in both the private sector and government seem to be completely irrational when it comes to making judgments about the use of chemicals in modern farming. Just as a whole generation of engineers and nuclear physicists were collectively seduced by the notional benefits of nuclear power, postwar chemists were seduced by the notional benefits of toxic chemicals in controlling agricultural pests and diseases. Both 'breakthroughs' were born of military research programmes, both received unquestioning government backing, and both rapidly developed such a power base in society that critical dissent was largely ignored.

The arrival of synthetic chemicals revolutionized postwar agriculture. Out went all the old pest-management techniques (such as crop rotation, mechanical weeding and utilizing natural predators) as farmers were encouraged by the purveyors of new 'miracle pesticides' to spray as often as necessary. The farming community was systematically colonized by the attitudes, language and behaviour of warfare, exhorted to triumph as valiantly over the enemy in our fields and forests as our armies had triumphed on the battlefields of the Second World War. Conquer, strike, destroy, eliminate – regardless of the fact, as Rachel Carson so poignantly testified, that all life would be 'caught in the crossfire'.

Both the variety and the volume of chemicals used rose dramatically. And notwithstanding a slight blip in the upward sales curves caused by public reaction to Rachel Carson's *Silent Spring*, that's pretty much the way it has stayed. Whereas levels of active ingredients in Europe have now fallen, sales have rocketed throughout Asia and South and Central America, and have remained more or less constant in the United States.

In an impeccably balanced book, *Nature Wars: People vs Pests* (1997), Mark Winston sums up the current situation:

> The extent and impact of our current dependence on pesticides for both agricultural and non-agricultural purposes is staggering. In 1993, 1.1 billion pounds of active pesticide ingredients were used in the United States, and 4.5 billion pounds world-wide. The US figure translates to about four pounds of pesticides for every man, woman and child in America. Considering that toxic dosages of most pesticides to humans are about $100,000^{th}$ to $1,000,000^{th}$ of a pound, that's a considerable amount of poison.

And to what effect? Astonishingly, actual numbers of pests on our farms have increased, largely as a result of increased resistance to the chemicals being used, and the fact that they have a tendency to wipe out the pests' natural predators as well as the pests themselves. David Pimentel of Cornell University has calculated that more than $500,000,000-worth of crops in the United States are lost every year because the pesticides kill off the natural enemies of the pest that is damaging the crop.

Developing Resistance

It is of course true that most pesticides used today are much less toxic than those developed in the aftermath of the Second World War. But it's only in the last ten years or so that we've begun to recognize the full range of impacts caused by their continuing use both in agriculture and in our homes and gardens. The environmental impact has been disastrous, and few have yet come to terms with the consequences of this non-stop toxic assault on human health. A shocking report from the World Health Organisation in 1989 made an informal guess at around one million cases of pesticide poisoning every year, resulting in twenty thousand deaths, largely in developing countries.

It's the combination of negative factors that makes this situation so startling. If pesticides were actually doing an effective job in managing pests, we might decide that the downstream costs of using pesticides on our health and environment were still justifiable – a reasonable trade-off. But the percentage of crops lost to pests globally has actually increased, from around 30 per cent in the 1940s to around 35 per cent in the 1990s. Even in America the figure has gone up from 7 per cent in the 1940s to 13 per cent by the early 1990s.

The phenomenon of resistance lies at the heart of this. Many pesticides are becoming less effective even as we see more of them in use. More than five hundred serious insect pests and a hundred weeds are now resistant to one or more pesticides, with the numbers continuing to grow. Every time a pesticide is used, a certain number of the target pest manage to survive, and even prosper, given that much of the competition has been exterminated. In time, they breed with other survivors, reinforcing the genetic resistance of their progeny. The farmer ends up needing to apply even more of the pesticide next time round, with even more insects becoming resistant. The metaphor of the pesticide treadmill is a telling one – and millions of farmers all around the world can't get off it.

All this has been understood by scientists for decades, as has the need to find alternatives:

> A truly extraordinary variety of alternatives to the chemical control of insects is available. Some are already in use, and have achieved brilliant success. Others are in the stage of laboratory testing. Still others are little more than ideas in the minds of imaginative scientists, waiting for the opportunity to put them to the test. Some of the most interesting of the recent work is concerned with ways of forging weapons from the insect's own life processes.

That was Rachel Carson in 1962. The pesticides treadmill is still whirring away. Most of the biological alternatives on which Carson and others pinned their hopes (including the use of pheromones and growth regulators, sterile insect releases, the introduction and enhancement of natural predators and pesticides, and so on) have proved problematic and disappointing. Integrated pest management (IPM) itself – once all the rage amongst advocates of alternative strategies – has delivered far fewer benefits than was initially hoped. Notwithstanding the occasional add-on use of biological controls, IPM is still a chemically driven rather than an ecologically driven approach to pest management.

Mark Winston in *Nature Wars* provides a compelling account of why this has happened. Not only have the alternatives proved too costly, they've also been too complicated to use. Instead of just slapping on the chemicals, biological control systems require much closer monitoring of pest populations, much deeper knowledge of the lifecycle of each individual pest species, and much more complex ways of administering and evaluating their use.

There was once a time when farmers had to be amateur scientists – ecologist, botanist, agronomist, chemist, entomologist, hydrologist, and meteorologist all rolled into one. One of the least recognized but most pernicious consequences of modern intensive farming is the systematic de-skilling that has gone on, with farmers handing over more and more of the responsibility for pest management to advisors and sales teams of the agro-chemical companies.

In the process, there's been a profound shift in our philosophical orientation towards the 'pests' that our modern farming systems have in fact done so much to encourage. As Rachel Carson said: 'The "control of nature" is a phrase conceived in arrogance, born of the Neanderthal age of biology and philosophy, when it was supposed that nature exists for the convenience of man.' Extermination has been the name of the game, rather than some kind of (albeit grudging) cohabitation. In the most ignorant and arrogant way imaginable, we've gone to war against nature itself, as Mark Winston explains:

> Our gravest mistake has been in setting a pest agenda that considers pests a problem that must be controlled rather than an integral part of nature that we should manage in effective, environmentally responsible ways. Ironically, by waging wars on pests that we cannot win, we have turned ourselves into nature's losers. The most important effect of our chosen role in nature as dominators rather than stewards has been to lose our sense of place in the biological world around us.

It is no coincidence that the principal long-term alternative to the chemical treadmill is the one that has most consistently reflected precisely that stewardship ethos. After decades in the doldrums, organic farming is at last coming into its own in both Europe and the United States. Consumers have started to recognize that if they want a guarantee of protection against chemical residues (let alone genetically modified ingredients), then the strictly regulated organic label is the only one they can trust. Farmers have started to recognize that they have to be more responsive to consumer demand, and that organic farming offers the best route off the pesticides treadmill. Equally significantly, environment organizations have at long last come to realize that organic farmers offer the best route to promoting biological diversity and environment-friendly management practices across the whole farm – not just in the odd hedgerow, copse or field margin.

In the process, one myth that can finally be nailed is the idea that organic farming is somehow 'unscientific' or backward-looking. Scientists employed by MAFF and the big agro-chemical companies have made an art form over the years of disparaging the quality of research into organic farming, paying scant regard to increasingly strong data about the advantages of organics. With almost the lowest percentage of land under organic production in the whole of Europe, the UK is now paying a heavy price for that irrational and deeply unscientific bias, reflected even now in MAFF's research budget.

The need for the best possible research is as great in organic farming as in any other farming system. Greater, indeed, if you accept the argument advanced here that, both philosophically and practically, organic farming provides the best relief from today's chemical dependency. Yet thousands of the best brains in agricultural research are employed primarily to crank out extra profits for agro-chemical and biotech companies, with just a few dozen labouring away in small, underfunded institutes to give organic farming the kind of research support that other farming methods have long taken for granted.

The idea that the research agenda in this most important of all areas is driven by anything other than the pursuit of private profit at the expense of public interest is intellectually bankrupt. Money talks, as well as smells. You can't always blame the individual scientists who end up prostituting their genius in this way, but you have to ask what sort of world it is that forces them to sell their intellectual talents for such anti-social and unsustainable purposes.

So is that all we need – an organic revolution to combat the tide of toxics that has swept the world since the 1950s? If it were just a question of getting farmers off their chemical treadmill, and filling those supermarket shelves with fresh, nutritious produce totally free of poisonous residues, then there would be real grounds for optimism. But it isn't.

Industrial Poisons

At exactly the same time as farmers in Europe and the United States started spreading their poisons over the land, industrialists were gearing up to unleash a parallel and equally lethal assault on our air, water and cities. Forty years on, we know a lot more about the real cost of a whole array of 'miracle' products like Chlorofluorocarbons (CFCs) and Polychlorinated bi-phenyls (PCBs). More than 75,000 synthetic chemicals are now on the market, with a thousand new ones coming on board every year. Only a fraction of these is ever properly tested (a maximum of 3 per cent have been thoroughly tested for their potential to cause cancer), despite the knowledge we now have of the way chemicals can interfere with our hormones, weaken the immune system, attach themselves to our chromosomes, disrupt the activity of certain enzymes, and so on. According to the US National Research Council, only 10 per cent of pesticides in common use have been adequately assessed for hazards of different kinds; nothing at all is known about 38 per cent, and the rest fall somewhere in between.

There are 5.8 billion people on planet Earth today. Race, gender, religion, sex orientation, language, wealth: these and many other things remind us of the startling diversity that characterizes *Homo sapiens*. But one thing we have in common: there's not a single human being anywhere on the face of the Earth who has not been touched in some way (however small) by that continuing chemical barrage. We all bear the mark of that forty-year experiment as an accumulation of persistent synthetic chemicals in our body fat, the consequences of which will be with us for another forty years or more.

In 1996, I read a book called *Our Stolen Future* by Theo Colborn, John Peterson Myers and Dianne Dumanowski. It had the same shattering effect on me as Rachel Carson's *Silent Spring* thirty years earlier. Subtitled *A Scientific Detective Story*, it recounts the history of Theo Colborn as she painstakingly amassed evidence of the effects of synthetic chemicals that 'mimic' certain hormones (the chemical messengers that carry information around our bodies) in a wide range of life forms – including humans. With legions of scientists and policy-makers understandably but forlornly obsessed with trying to identify and 'mitigate' the damage caused by cancer-causing chemicals, she came to realize that we had been simply 'blind-sided' by a very different array of chemicals, capable of disrupting the endocrine or reproductive system in any organism. At minute concentrations. The development of the embryo is often assumed to be controlled exclusively by genes, but it is our hormones that switch genes on and off at that crucial stage. 'Genes may be the keyboard, but hormones compose the tune.' Disrupting that tune can have devastating consequences later in life.

Scientists have identified more than fifty chemicals – many of them widespread in the environment – that disrupt the reproductive system in one way or another. They include familiar suspects like PCBs, DDT and a number of different dioxins, as well as an array of less well known chemicals that may ultimately prove to be far more dangerous.

Colborn's investigation started with the ecological work that she was doing around the Great Lakes, and led her to gather data on aberrant reproductive behaviour in scores of different creatures, from alligators with abnormally small penises to herring gulls that couldn't rear any young, from hermaphrodite polar bears and beluga whales to frogs with extra limbs, missing eyes and even sprouting tails.

Based on the warnings from wildlife and lab animals, what kind of problems should we expect? Hormonally active synthetic chemicals can damage the reproductive system, alter the nervous system and brain, and impair the immune system. Animals contaminated by these chemicals show various behavioural effects, including aberrant mating behaviour and increased parental neglect of nests. Synthetic chemicals can derail the normal expression of sexual characteristics of animals, in some cases masculinizing females and feminizing males. Some animal studies indicate that exposure to hormonally active chemicals prenatally or in adulthood increases vulnerability to hormone-responsive cancers, such as malignancies in the breast, prostate, ovary and uterus.

Knowing that hormones guide development in basically the same way in all mammals, Colborn started to ask whether the same effects could be identified in humans. She and her colleagues amassed evidence that confirmed this, evidence that had previously never been put together.

Most controversially of all, Theo Colborn and her team hypothesized a link between exposure to these chemicals in the womb and increased behavioural disorder and learning disabilities in schoolchildren. Between 6 and 10 per cent of American children under the age of thirteen are said to be suffering some kind of hyperactivity or attention deficit, and psychologists are unable to agree on a convincing explanation for this growing phenomenon. Colborn even went so far as to speculate at one stage that current levels of contamination could impair average mental development enough to cause a significant loss in measurable IQ.

At a time when more and more children are prescribed powerful drugs, such as Ritalin, to control their behaviour, one might imagine that so dramatic a hypothesis would have seized public attention. But it didn't. And although the number of scientists concerned about the impact of persistent synthetic chemicals on our reproductive systems is growing all the time, it has yet to cross that indefinable threshold between scientific obscurity and scientific celebrity.

It makes an interesting contrast with another related health issue: falling sperm counts. It takes something quite special to make a predominantly male scientific establishment sit up and take notice, and there's nothing quite like a potential threat to our evolutionary purpose to achieve that. In the September 1992 issue of the *British Medical Journal*, Dr Niels Skakkebaek (Head of the Department of Growth and Reproduction at the University Hospital in Copenhagen) reported that the average male sperm count, based on 61 different studies in 20 countries and involving 15,000 men, had dropped 45 per cent from an average of 113 million sperm per millilitre of semen in 1940 to just 66 million in 1990. Moreover, the number of men with extremely low sperm counts (of less than 20 million) had tripled from 6 per cent to 18 per cent during the same period.

Consternation on all sides – and a lot of very hostile criticism of both Skakkebaek's methodology and his conclusions. But several subsequent studies (including some carried out by his most trenchant critics) have confirmed his original findings. If it's a trend, with sperm counts continuing to fall by roughly the same amount year on year, a thirty-year-old man in 2005 would have a sperm count of around one quarter of a thirty-year-old man in 1955. Whichever way you look at it, that's scary, although it's only fair to say that other studies have contradicted these findings, concluding that there's really nothing to worry about.

So the debate is still raging about how to account for these startling developments. What is the balance between possible damage done to the foetus in the womb and possible damage to the child, adolescent or adult through exposure during its lifetime to environmental pollutants? In 1993, Niels Skakkebaek and Richard Sharpe of the Medical Research Council's Reproductive Biology Unit published a paper in *The Lancet* suggesting that falling sperm counts and other abnormalities in men were being caused by increased exposure to certain oestrogens in the womb. They quoted the now infamous DES scandal – as many as three million women in the 1950s and 1960s were prescribed a synthetic oestrogen called Diethylstilbestrol (DES) to help prevent miscarriages, resulting in a much higher than average incidence of deformed penises, undescended testicles and lower sperm counts in their sons and a number of supporting animal studies. Moreover, they asked, if falling sperm counts were caused by chemical pollution later in life, why was it that the phenomenon was occurring only in younger men, and not in older men subject to the same contamination? Niels Skakkebaek came up with one further finding: the lower the sperm count, the higher the incidence of testicular cancer and genital defects. In Denmark, testicular cancer has tripled in just twenty-five years; in former East Germany, it is eleven times more common in men born in 1965 than in those born sixty years earlier.

Testicular cancer is just one of several kinds of cancer increasing in incidence even as the number of deaths they cause is falling, due to more effective diagnosis and treatment. Half of all cancers occur among people living in the industrialized world, even though they account for only 20 per cent of the world's population. The incidence of cancer in the United States doubled between 1950 and 1991 – or to put it another way, 'in 1950, a cancer diagnosis was the expected fate of about 25 per cent of all Americans, while today about 40 per cent of Americans will contract the disease some time within their life span.'

Cancer and Chemicals

These are just some of the statistics I have gleaned from Sandra Steingraber's extraordinary book, *Living Downstream* (1998). This was given to me by a close colleague just a couple of months after my mother's death from lung cancer, making it emotionally turbulent reading. Steingraber herself is a 'recovered cancer victim, from one of those cancer families', and a worthy successor to Carson in her dogged forensic determination and calm, campaigning compassion. As with Theo Colborn's *Our Stolen Future*, it's the kind of book which sets me thinking about the impact it must have on her scientific colleagues, and the way in which they may come to reappraise the value of their own work. Especially within the cancer research industry.

For the truth of it is that links between cancer and what has been described as 'the growing chemicalization of the human economy' have never been systematically investigated. Only in 1994 did the US National Cancer Advisory Board call for a co-ordinated investigation of industrial chemicals and pesticides as potential causes of cancer, and then only because the flow of small-scale, often local studies had started to throw up evidence that even the cancer establishment couldn't ignore.

Take hazardous waste sites, for example. Since the late 1950s, 750 million tons of toxic chemical wastes have been disposed of in tens of thousands of waste dumps across the United States. According to the Environmental Protection Agency, 32,645 of these need active clean-up, including around 1400 so-called 'Superfund sites' – the worst offenders. Forty million people live within four miles, about six kilometres, of one of these sites. For years, there have been accounts (both scientific and anecdotal) of increased rates of cancer and ill health around waste dumps, but only in 1992 did the Agency for Toxic Substances concede that 'a variety of types of cancer are encountered more often than would be expected in human populations exposed to contaminants and waste sites.'

Similar concerns have been raised in Britain. A team led by Helen Dolk, an environmental epidemiologist at the London School of Hygiene and Tropical Medicine, studied twenty-one landfill sites in Britain and Europe. The headline conclusion of their work was stark: mothers living within three kilometres, or two miles, of such sites run up to a 33 per cent higher risk of having babies suffering a range of congenital abnormalities. The UK government has yet to respond formally to their report, but has commissioned a two-year investigation into the possible impacts of these 'toxic time-bombs'.

There are few areas of science that are more complex or controversial. Cancer experts are deeply divided amongst themselves about the percentage of cancers that can be attributed to environmental factors. Using the broadest of broad-brush approaches, the World Health Organization (WHO) has concluded that 'at least 80 per cent of all cancer is attributable to environmental influence'. It arrived at that statistic by analysing cancer mortality figures from death certificates in seventy different countries and comparing countries with the highest and lowest rates. The lowest rate provides a benchmark which is assumed to be more or less constant on account of hereditary and other factors; the highest rates include all of those plus all those cancers attributable to both environmental factors (everything we involuntarily come into contact with) and lifestyle factors (everything we choose to come into contact with). The variation between the highest and the lowest is quite reasonably reckoned to represent the percentage of cancers that can be attributed to 'the environment' – and 'environment' here, for the WHO, embraces both environmental and lifestyle factors.

This method of calculation is fiercely opposed by those who dismiss the whole idea of widespread environmental carcinogens, talking instead of a figure at the other end of the scale – around 2 per cent instead of 80 per cent. It probably goes without saying that many of these people have links with the chemical industry. What's more, Steingraber makes short work of the idea that we shouldn't in any case be too worried at such a low figure:

Let's assume for the sake of argument that this lowest value 2 per cent is absolutely correct. Two per cent means that 10,940 people in the United States die each year from environmentally caused cancers. This is more than the number of women who die each year from hereditary breast cancer – an issue that has launched multi-million dollar research initiatives. This is more than the number of children and teenagers killed each year by firearms – an issue that is considered a matter of national shame. It is more than three times the number of non-smokers estimated to die each year of lung cancer caused by exposure to second-hand smoke – a problem so serious it warranted sweeping changes in laws governing air quality in public spaces. It is the annual equivalent of wiping out a small city. It is thirty funerals every day.

For Steingraber, this is a form of homicide.

But not, it would seem, for the cancer research establishments, spearheaded by the National Cancer Institute in America and the Imperial Cancer Research Fund in the UK. They continue to spend astronomical amounts of money pursuing 'magic bullet' cures or treatment regimes, apparently fixated on the notion that if they can chuck enough money at the problem, then the cancer epidemic will be sorted. To achieve this wholly unachievable goal, they leap dextrously from one bandwagon to the next, depending on where the money seems to be flowing most freely.

The latest bandwagon, predictably, is genetically driven. The assumption is that if we can only identify the genes in which any defect will lead to certain kinds of cancer, then millions of people's lives will be improved or even saved. Biotech companies are hard at it identifying (and instantly patenting) such genes, with the prospect of huge revenue streams from diagnostic testing. For instance, two separate genes have already been identified for breast cancer. But should this give women any cause for comfort? As cancer expert Ross Hume Hall puts it (in the *Ecologist*):

So while lawyers, court cases and the lure of big money from diagnostic testing swirl around the breast cancer genes, what about women and their risk of breast cancer? The two genes are connected only with hereditary breast cancers – 5 to 10 per cent of all cases. And what good does such a test do? If the test shows a woman carries a defective gene, there is a limit to what can be done. In many ways, this highly sophisticated research does increase our understanding of human biology. What is of concern however is the way the medical-industrial complex uses such research. They would have us believe that because of various findings, such as cancer genes, the cure lies just around the corner. The truth is, however, it doesn't make much difference if a cure ever emerges. The search is a splendid money-generator.

In March 1998, the *Ecologist* brought out a special issue devoted to the politics of cancer, exposing the lies and half-truths of what it called 'the medical-industrial complex'. Its case was succinctly summed up by editor Edward Goldsmith:

Cancer is now a disease that afflicts one out of three people, and everybody knows in their hearts, on the basis of countless studies and from the experience of vulnerable groups, that the main causes are: exposure to carcinogenic chemicals and ionising radiation – from medical X-rays, nuclear tests and radioactive emissions from nuclear installations. However, the Cancer Establishment will not admit it. Nor of course will the ever more powerful pharmaceutical and nuclear industries that fund nearly all the research on the causes of cancer, and make quite sure that the present cancer epidemic is attributed to anything except exposure to chemicals and radioactivity.

For anyone interested not just in cancer but in the debate about the role of science in modern society, this issue (and the *Ecologist* magazine generally) provides the kind of detailed critique of which we find all too little in the mainstream media. It may be no coincidence that the *Ecologist* carries no advertisements from large companies (and is thus independent of this source of revenue), whereas dozens of magazines that purport to tell you the truth about health and environmental issues could not survive without advertising income.

Moreover, when one strips bare the intimate links that connect notionally 'independent' cancer research with the interests of big business and government, the idea of 'value-free science' in this particular area becomes entirely untenable. The bottom line is that it makes good business to go on pouring billions of dollars into better ways of dealing with people once they've contracted cancer, rather than focusing investment on ways to prevent people contracting cancer in the first place. That governments continue to reinforce that particular 'bottom line' is deeply cynical. So as the advertisements for those UK cancer charities get to work on your heartstrings, just bear in mind that if we spent even a fraction of the money raised eliminating some of the probable causes of cancer rather than elaborating the cures, the level of human suffering would be dramatically reduced. Particularly for children. One of the most chilling accounts in *Living Downstream* is Steingraber's description of one particular study of more than eight hundred breast-feeding mothers in North Carolina. Research found that the concentration of organochlorine chemicals in breast milk decreased dramatically over the course of lactation and with the number of children nursed:

> Organochlorine contaminants are not easily expunged from our tissues. Their sharp decline in concentration over the course of breast-feeding, therefore, represents the movement of accumulated toxins from mother to child. It signifies that during the intimate act of nursing, a burden of public poisons (insect killers, electrical insulating fluids, industrial solvents, and incinerator residues) is shifted from one generation into the tiny bodies of the next.

The contrast between that physical reality and the aspirational rhetoric of sustainable development ('not cheating on our children') becomes almost impossibly difficult to live with. But this is by no means the only area where the rich language of inter-generational equity turns to bitter gall in your mouth when you look hard at the mass trespass our generation is making on the rights and interests of future generations.

CHAPTER 5

CLIMATE SCIENCE

Tens of thousands of people die every year because of exposure to pesticides and other toxic chemicals. And similar numbers will go on dying every year for quite some time to come. By contrast, it would be extremely difficult to demonstrate that anyone had yet died from changes in the climate specifically brought about through pollution from our industrial economies. And yet, slowly but surely, the international community is laying the foundations of a global plan to address the challenge of climate change. I believe this has much to do with the case I shall be making in this chapter: that, as you survey the whole range of environmental issues, climate change may very well turn out to be the one where the science process used becomes a model for handling other global environmental impacts.

Few environmental activists would agree with that judgment. They see the climate change process as an agonizingly and irresponsibly slow one, riven by apparently endless disputes between scientists on different sides of the climate change divide. In fact, those delays are less to do with the science of climate change than with its somewhat grubbier politics.

Firstly, what do we actually know about climate change? We know that for billions of years natural emissions of water vapour, carbon dioxide and other gases have helped maintain the temperature of the Earth within a range at which life can exist. They act like a greenhouse, trapping the sun's heat within the atmosphere.

We know that there have been both dramatic changes in temperature and climate, and long periods of relative climatic stability since the earliest records we have. Both the 'Greenhouse Effect' and climate change are therefore completely natural phenomena which would be going on in their own way even if the human species hadn't emerged as the dominant species on Earth.

We know that levels of carbon dioxide have gradually been building up in the atmosphere from pre-industrial levels of around 280 parts per million (ppm) to 360 ppm today, and are likely to reach 560 ppm (a doubling of pre-industrial levels) by 2040. We know that this will inevitably (but to an uncertain extent) reinforce (or 'enhance') the background Greenhouse Effect.

We know almost for sure that this additional carbon dioxide is coming from human (or 'anthropogenic') activities, particularly from the burning of fossil fuels – coal, oil and gas – and the continuing destruction of the Earth's forests.

And we know that the climate is changing in a myriad of different ways and different places all around the world. Local and regional climate records testify to 'the hottest this' and 'the wettest that', to unprecedented droughts here and unprecedented flooding there, to an accelerating proliferation of unseasonal and uncharacteristic effects that is turning the people of every nation in the world into the kind of weather-gossips for which the British alone were once justifiably renowned.

By way of hard-edged knowledge, which it's all but impossible for anyone to disagree with, that's just about it. Beyond that, everything else is rather less clear-cut (in terms of measurable effects, let alone causes), or still firmly in the zone of 'things that might happen' according to a bewildering variety of models, forecasts, simulations and exercises in rudimentary guesswork.

And that's exactly the problem about climate change. We're talking about hugely complex natural and man-made systems; about time-scales that make the average politician blench with horror; about feedback loops which it may not be possible for us to predict before they have actually fed back; about innumerable different scientific disciplines, most of which are barely aware of the existence of other disciplines; and about uncertainty piled on uncertainty until people begin to wonder if there's anything left firm enough to hang on to at all.

But the sheer weight of the 'probables' and the 'possibles' in terms of potentially devastating impacts on agriculture, sea-levels, biological diversity, disease, storm-damage and so on, has persuaded the vast majority of scientists involved in research in this area that action must be taken now in advance of the kind of definitive cause-and-effect evidence that is usually required by politicians before action is taken. However falteringly, the Precautionary Principle is clearly evident in many of the decisions now being taken.

It's interesting to speculate how much this relative progress (relative, for instance, to the almost total lack of progress on eliminating carcinogens and other toxic chemicals) has to do with the ownership of those research and decision-making processes. Research in climate change is largely government-driven, with the lion's share of research budgets coming (directly or indirectly) from government departments. With both toxic chemicals (dealt with in the last chapter) and genetic engineering (the subject of the next chapter), the contrast couldn't be greater. In both these instances, the science is owned (literally and metaphorically) by a small number of very large companies promoting a wide range of different products. Much of the research is commercially confidential, never sees the light of day, and is carried out with the sole intent of generating future revenue streams. Nothing wrong with that in itself, of course, but it raises a substantial question mark over both the quality and the transparency of the research work done, especially as the companies involved have pretty much co-opted and shaped the respective regulatory processes to suit their own commercial purposes.

For those with enough patience to enjoy it, by the way, it's a nice irony that the real megabucks in the twenty-first century will be made by businesses managing the transition from a carbon-based to a solar-based economy. This constitutes a low-risk, high-return, consumer and environment-friendly commercial revolution, in contrast to the high-risk, average-return, highly controversial world of genetic engineering. Which inevitably causes one to question the entrepreneurial intelligence of politicians in both Britain and the United States as they enthuse so indiscriminately about a genetically modified future, while continuing to treat renewable energy as a minor niche market.

Consensus and Dissent

There are two things of real importance when considering the science of climate change. In the first place, it's uncommon to discover such overwhelming scientific consensus on such a controversial set of issues. This is important; in such a fiercely contested area, numbers really do count as far as politicians are concerned when trying to sort the wheat from the chaff.

Secondly, and equally importantly, such a consensus provides absolutely no guarantee that the science underpinning it is correct, and for many dissenting and wholly reputable scientists (I'll get on to the disreputable ones a bit later), the fact that so powerful a consensus has emerged is in itself a source of concern. Like everyone else, scientists know a good bandwagon when they see one. Although it's clearly a politically motivated slander to suggest that climate change scientists are simply toeing the consensus line in order to attract lucrative research grants, one can only regret that in some places it does indeed appear to have become politically incorrect to question the consensus about climate change.

The dissenters pursue four main lines of attack. Firstly, they continue to question whether the world really is getting hotter. As each year's average temperature is logged (with 1998 the hottest year on record, and the 1990s the hottest decade for 600 years), it gets harder and harder to make much mileage out of this. All the more so now that satellite data used by dissenters to challenge the validity of computer models have been shown to have been incorrectly calculated.

Secondly, dissenters argue that natural factors (such as sunspot activity or volcanic eruptions) are far more likely to be causing changes in the climate than increased levels of CO_2 and other greenhouse gases in the atmosphere. They argue that there's a strong correlation in the historical record between average global temperatures and changes in the sun's brightness – and they may or may not be right. Even if they are, what we're then looking at is an 'additive effect', with climate change part natural and part man-made. The problem is that there's not a lot we can do about the temperature of the sun and volcanic eruptions, whereas we can do something about the man-made element, however big or small that may be.

Thirdly, the dissenters have tried to argue that the costs of tackling climate change early will be so much greater than just waiting for it to happen and then doing something about it, that it is irresponsible of governments to be doing anything before they absolutely have to. The arguments and economic calculations used to justify this position are so bizarre and so patently rigged to confirm their own prejudices as not to warrant further mention in a book about science.

Lastly, if all else fails, dissenters fall back on an anguished critique about the degree to which computer models are being used to justify policy recommendations. They have a point here – along the familiar lines of garbage-in, garbage-out. However, the computer models are getting not just more powerful but also qualitatively better (i.e. able to handle a wider range of variables more authoritatively), and correlations between the computer models and empirical data are getting stronger, though there's still a long way to go. As it happens, there's very little going on in the 'virtual greenhouse' to give the dissenters much succour in their arguments.

And those models do make for scary bedtime reading. In the run-up to the Climate Change Conference in Buenos Aires in November 1998, a number of reports hit the desks of UK ministers. One was from the Hadley Centre for Climate Change, using the world's largest super-computer involved in climate modelling. Among other things, it suggested that temperatures will rise by up to 6°C by the end of the next century; that the number of people on the coasts subject to flooding will rise to 100 million by 2050 and 200 million by 2080; that another 30 million people will be hungry in 50 years' time; that an extra 170 million people will live in countries with extreme water shortages.

Another report, from the Institute of Terrestrial Ecology in Edinburgh, involving a team of researchers from the UK, US, Spain and Austria, suggested that climate change could put 18 per cent more of

the population of Africa at risk of hunger by the 2050s, with an antici-
pated shortfall of 90 million tonnes of food, increasing the number of
people at risk of hunger by 30 million.

Another, from Oxford's Climate Impact Programme, drew up four
scenarios of potential changes in future UK weather patterns, none of
which made very rosy reading. It was suggested that temperatures
could rise by as much as 3°C in the UK over the next century, increasing the frequency of floods, severe winter gales and heatwaves.
And yet another, from the government's five senior advisors in this
area, simply said that they would be well advised to be guided by all
of the above!

Lard into that rich mix periodic warnings from a growing number
of scientists that the incidence of wind storms (hurricanes, typhoons,
cyclones, etc.) is increasing and will continue to increase as average
sea temperatures rise in the tropics, and you can understand why
European politicians head off to these international conferences with
rumpled brows and the kind of campaigning fervour which was once
the hallmark of Friends of the Earth and Greenpeace.

These long-term projections are, of course, constantly checked
against the short-term climate record. It's a fact that the twelve hottest
years in recorded history have occurred since 1980. But is that a
pattern that can be attributed to anthropogenic climate change, or just
one of those periodic warm spells caused by natural factors?

In this respect, it's not just the big picture stuff that makes the prevailing hypothesis look increasingly convincing. In the UK scientists
tracking climate impacts on biological diversity have revealed an extraordinary pattern of impacts on individual species: Mediterranean fish
species turning up off our coasts for the first time in recorded history;
butterflies emerging from their chrysalis a fortnight earlier than they
have done for years; migratory birds arriving earlier, staying longer,
and sometimes even over-wintering; resident birds laying their eggs
several weeks earlier; plants, shrubs and trees flowering earlier. And
spare a thought for the unfortunate Lucky, Britain's sole surviving pool
frog, which croaked its last in a south London garden, killed off by the
unseasonably warm winter weather that disrupted its hibernation.

This catalogue of micro-impacts has stimulated the usual 'end-of-the-world-is-nigh' reaction from environmentalists, who have long argued that the pace of policy change in response to such phenomena is inadequate. They point in particular to the very modest targets set under the Kyoto Protocol for reductions in carbon dioxide and other greenhouse gases. When set against the scientific evidence, which indicates that we need to be aiming at a 60 per cent cut in these gases within two or three decades if we are to avoid serious climatic destabilization, the aggregate Kyoto target (of a 5.2 per cent cut by 2012 at the latest) does indeed leave a lot to be desired.

And there are still huge problems with the Protocol. It's by no means certain that it will be ratified. With a lame duck president in Bill Clinton, opposition in the United States will not be won over easily, and Vice-President Gore is now so intent on his own presidential campaign that potentially unpopular issues like the environment will be given a very low priority. Developing countries have made their accession to the Protocol dependent on the rich world having done enough first – a difficult one to demonstrate at the moment. And even if that target is met, global emissions will still rise to 30 per cent above 1990 levels by 2010.

So the politics will undoubtedly continue to constrain the kind of progress that now needs to be made. But in this area, as in no other, it's possible to separate out the politics from the science. At each of the international conferences which drive the climate change agenda forward, there's a symbolic moment when the scientists complete their deliberations and sign off on a summary of their 'best bet recommendations' in the light of the latest research; this is then handed over to the politicians – who promptly start to duck and weave and find every which way of avoiding the implications of what the scientists are telling them!

But the foundations have been laid. Again, relative to most other international environmental science processes, this one is pretty secure. Tribute must be paid here to the Intergovernmental Panel on Climate Change (IPCC) that presides over the process. This body was set up in 1988 at the behest of the United Nations General Assembly to advise governments, and now involves more than 1800 scientists from all around the world, engaged in one way or another in elucidating the science of climate change. Through a number of working groups, these scientists move forward by consensus with a highly active peer-group review process in place, not just to eliminate the 'wild cards', but to give everyone an opportunity to bring their views to bear on the debate. It is this process (constituting 'sound science', even by the strictest definition) which makes it hard for dissenters to portray the response to climate change as a wicked anti-capitalist plot dreamed up by rabid environmental activists who have somehow managed to lure governments the world over into their evil snares.

Having been given the remit to advise governments, the advice the IPCC has given them is that 'on the balance of probability' we are now witnessing 'discernible climate change due to human activities.' And in perhaps the most radical conclusion of all (and one which it has seen no reason to tone down, let alone withdraw in the light of new evidence), the IPCC stated in 1990 that greenhouse gas emissions would need to be reduced by 60 per cent just as soon as possible.

The combination of high-level advice, ground-level data, and increasingly authoritative projections, makes it difficult for governments to avert their eyes from what's actually happening, inconvenient and unwelcome though these findings undoubtedly are. Having set up the IPPC specifically to tell them what needs to be done, it would be the height of collective political irresponsibility to base their decisions on any other interpretation of the data; any 'prevailing consensus' is only as resilient as its ability to withstand fierce and continual criticism, in both the detail and on the whole case, but it gives governments as solid a bedrock for introducing policies and committing funds as they are ever going to get in the face of such persistent and unavoidable uncertainty.

The success of this process shouldn't be overstated. Non-governmental organizations have constantly suggested that the IPCC is too cautious in its interpretation of the data, and in its recommendations to governments. By contrast, some governments (particularly the US administration) complain that evidence which conflicts with the consensus is given insufficient attention. They have pointed to the IPCC's inherent tendency to overstate the degree of confidence they have in the findings, which in many instances, by definition, can be little more than guesstimates.

This charge has been accepted by many leading climate change scientists, and there is now a move towards a more 'consistent assessment and reporting of uncertainties.' A ranking has been proposed, all the way through from 'virtually certain' (99 per cent sure), 'confident' (90 per cent) and 'probable' (66 per cent), to 'questionable' (33 per cent), 'unlikely' (10 per cent) and 'very unlikely' (1 per cent). With 'possible' safely in the middle, no doubt.

Responsible scientists have no option but to reflect this kind of unavoidable uncertainty in the way they report issues and advise politicians – yet without losing the overall plot. The climate change briefing to the UK cabinet, written by Sir Robert May, the government's Chief Scientist, just before the Kyoto Conference in 1997, is a classic of its kind, summarizing the science and weighing the balance of probabilities, but leaving his political masters in no doubt as to where their responsibilities lay. It is a style epitomized by the work of Sir John Houghton (a former Head of the Meteorological Office in the UK who now chairs one of the IPCC's key Working Groups), whose calm voice of reason has done so much to encourage politicians not to put off difficult decisions any longer.

Bought Science

But uncertainty of this kind can be used in a very different way by those scientists for whom the pursuit of truth has long since become an academic self-indulgence. The climate change debate has thrown up more than its fair share of so-called 'independent scientific experts', who exploit genuine uncertainty to cast doubt by allusion and by extension on those aspects of the debate where there is now very little remaining uncertainty.

Unfortunately, the behaviour of some of them is a lot worse than that, especially in the United States, where a substantial number of scientists are employed by front organizations working on behalf of big business or right-wing political interests specifically to rubbish good environmental science (not just on climate change) and to impugn the motivation and credentials of environmental scientists. 'Bought science' has been an ugly and corrupt element in this debate for many years, provoking comment not just from campaigners and environmental organizations, but from scientists themselves (who are particularly irritated at the amount of coverage these front organizations get on the basis of spurious 'scientific papers' which are rarely published in any reputable scientific journal and therefore never subject to the kind of peer review process which underpins the IPCC), and even politicians. I shall never forget John Gummer, as UK Secretary of State for the Environment, inveighing against 'the abuse of science' in a memorable TV interview in 1996 when the media had latched on to yet another sensationalist bit of knocking copy.

For those who remain unconvinced that these are the depths to which some scientists really will stoop, perusal of two painstakingly researched books on the anti-environment movement in the US and around the world would bring considerable benefits: Andy Rowell's *Green Backlash* (1996) and Sharon Beder's *Global Spin* (1997).

There are many well-meaning but essentially naïve proponents of the notion of 'value-free science' who are, to be sure, vaguely discomfited by this kind of abuse of science, but who tend to dismiss it airily as 'not real science anyway'. That, of course, won't do. Abuse of this kind is engrained in the very structure of contemporary science, where big business increasingly calls the shots on research agendas, intellectual property rights, confidentiality and so on. Were it not for the impeccable credentials of the IPCC process, groups like the Global Climate Coalition (a powerful pseudo-scientific front for the world's energy-intensive industries which has been particularly influential in the US) and its scientific stooges would have exercised an even more malign influence on the tortuous decision-making process surrounding climate change.

Environmentalists remain deeply concerned at the way in which this anti-scientific backlash has slowed down a more progressive agenda for environmental clean-up and reform. Many have been so disgusted at the historical and deeply-rooted marginalization of environmental issues by some multinational companies that they dismiss out of hand any measures taken by those companies to respond to what environmental science now tells them. This is understandable, but refusing on ideological grounds to differentiate between good corporate practice and bad corporate practice is as foolish – in a fundamentalist kind of way – as refusing to differentiate between good science and bad science.

Many global companies are increasingly anxious about their reputation, their scientific credibility, and their overall 'licence to operate' in a world rather less star-struck by their technical virtuosity and wealth-creating beneficence than it once was. When BP (now BP Amoco) quit the Global Climate Coalition in 1997, it had less to do with pressure from environmentalists than with a sense of what they owed themselves (as a science- and engineering-based company) and their shareholders in terms of integrity and proper scientific process. Shell duly followed suit a year later, and Ford in December 1999. BP Amoco's leadership role and its readiness to accept the 'best-bet', precautionary approach of the IPCC, has impressed even the most cynical of environmental campaigners.

And what have they got to lose anyway? Companies like BP Amoco and Shell have precisely the kind of engineering capabilities and global reach which will put them in pole position as the world slowly but surely moves over from carbon-based energy strategies to renewable energy strategies. There will be no less demand for pioneering, cutting-edge science in fashioning a sustainable future than there has been historically in overcoming scarcity through industrial development. And no fewer opportunities for turning handsome profits in the process.

Which is what makes it so frustrating that it takes so long to move from presentation of an increasingly powerful (if not yet irrefutable) scientific case through to strategic policy response and operational implementation. It's not as if we've got forever: the 'warning signals' we're picking up now will have been triggered by emissions of CO_2 and other greenhouse gases at least a decade ago – that's how long it takes for an 'enhanced greenhouse effect' to work through as a feed-back mechanism into higher temperatures and other climatic effects.

Business can adapt. So can we. Costs will almost certainly be far lower than those suggested in the nightmare scenarios of those with a clear vested interest in painting the gloomiest picture possible – they always are. Necessity is still the mother of invention, and we're on the brink of a veritable explosion in technological and engineering inven-tiveness. After all, energy is wonderful stuff, liberating and wealth-creating. We want more of it, not less of it, but without the damaging side-effects that now threaten to undermine the prospects of the whole of humankind.

The identification of an enhanced greenhouse effect ('the mother and father of all environmental issues') is spurring us on to rethink the long-term shape of the global economy. For whatever we do now in the name of addressing climate change should be done anyway – even without that stimulus – if long-term sustainability is really our game plan. I shall revisit such a radical and subversive notion in Chapter 7, after a brief excursion into the genetically modified future that awaits us all.

CHAPTER 6

THE GENETICS REVOLUTION

'Revolution' is a much abused word, especially when applied to processes of change that are merely going a little faster than usual. But in the case of genetics today, it is the only word that conveys both the scale and speed with which our lives are about to be transformed.

Things are moving simultaneously on many different fronts, with the genes of every single organism (from the human being down to the lowliest bacteria) available for research, manipulation and commercial exploitation. There are no limits to the aspirations of those who are driving this revolution, and very few external limits to help define what is or isn't appropriate. Though they are among the brightest people in the world, there's not much to distinguish the frontier mentality of some of today's gene pioneers from that of Wild Bill Hickock and friends who opened up the West. There are rich (i.e. patentable) pickings out there, so let's go get 'em!

With astonishing technical virtuosity, the genetics revolution is pushing out into unknown territory. Forget genetically modified soya, maize or tomatoes, and focus instead on vaccine-producing potatoes, plants that 'manufacture' biodegradable plastics, 'smart plants' that will signal to farmers when they're being attacked by pests or need more water, cloned trees that grow faster, get felled more easily and produce pulp that almost melts in your mouth, microbes that gobble up radio-active and toxic waste, flowers that won't bloom until triggered by a special spray, and pigs, sheep and God-knows-what other creatures producing a wide range of drugs or chemicals for industrial use. While we're worrying ourselves silly about labelling GM soya, the brains of our genetic revolutionaries are buzzing with ideas for literally thousands of genetically engineered products over the next ten to fifteen years.

One can therefore sympathize with those charged with the responsibility of regulating these headstrong pioneers. No sooner do we work out how to handle one 'breakthrough', than the next is upon us, swamping the limited government machinery set up to protect society from any damaging consequences of the genetics revolution. These processes are invariably two or three steps behind the game, and sometimes not in the same game at all. Regulatory problems have been exacerbated by politicians in the US and UK sharing the biotech industry's pioneering zeal, talking up the great marvels that await us, as if life today without these marvels is completely inadequate. They seem to have learned little from the history of earlier technological 'miracles'.

As the Prince of Wales has so cogently argued in his highly influential contributions to this debate, part of the problem is that the ethical horse has already well and truly bolted. Decision-making processes are so driven by short-term commercial considerations that even to raise ethical and spiritual concerns is portrayed by some as a sign of intellectual inadequacy. To assert (as Prince Charles has done) that today's genetic revolutionaries are 'taking mankind into realms that belong to God and to God alone' induces near apoplectic rage in the boardrooms of biotech companies like Novartis or Monsanto.

It's impossible to talk about GM crops without turning the spotlight on Monsanto. It bestrides the scene in terms of both the number of GM products under development and crop acreage. It also dominates media coverage on account of the very high-profile stance it has taken on a number of controversial issues. And its Chairman and Chief Executive, Bob Shapiro, has sought to justify everything his company is doing as serving the cause of sustainability.

The origins of this go back to the early 1990s when US farmers first started using Monsanto's GM soya. The GM soya was streamed in with ordinary soya, making it impossible for food processors to know what they were using, impossible for retailers to come up with any informative labelling, and impossible for consumers to know what they were buying and eating.

Long before this became a high-profile environmental and consumer issue, Monsanto was warned by food retailers and processors across Europe that such an inept and arrogant course of action could easily inflame what was then a relatively calm area of public debate. Zeneca's GM tomato paste (clearly labelled for all to see) had caused hardly a stir. NGOs (non-governmental organisations) were in fact struggling to make much of an impact with their anti-GM campaigns, either with politicians or the general public. However, having faced next to no opposition in the United States, Monsanto ignored the warnings, as concerns about free choice, bullying US companies, and 'genetic pollution' hit the media headlines. Monsanto is now routinely stigmatized by the rest of the industry for having set back the 'biotech cause' by several years. Commentators in the US are talking openly of the company having to sell off its GM business in order to protect shareholder value.

Sticking all the blame on Monsanto may be a little harsh. You can never tell what combination of external factors is ultimately responsible for pitching an issue over that threshold which divides relatively calm, rational scientific discourse from media-hyped, polarized confrontation. But once it's over that threshold, science often loses out to extremism, fear and ignorance, and dragging a complex and potentially emotional issue like genetic engineering back down to earth again may prove next to impossible in the short term. The UK government's announcement in October 1999 that there would be a formal three-year freeze on the commercial planting of GM crops was a tacit acknowledgement that it would take at least that long to bring the debate back down to what it considers a 'rational base' – let alone to restore trust.

Cultural differences between Europe and the United States have played a significant part in this process. Industry leaders struggle to explain why it is that most Americans seem to have taken GM in their stride, while most Europeans (and often their governments) are up in arms. While Americans use soothing vocabulary, such as 'transgenic plants' (which sound as if they wouldn't be out of place in an upmarket beauty clinic), we talk of 'Frankenstein foods'.

One of the most commonly quoted differences is the fact that the average American consumer continues to have trust in the relevant regulatory bodies, particularly the Food and Drug Administration (FDA), whereas here in the UK (and to a lesser extent elsewhere in Europe) there is really very little trust at all. And at one level, the FDA and the US Environmental Protection Agency do seem to have exercised a fairly rigorous approach: the first field tests were stringently controlled; licences for new GM crops are still difficult to get; and, as yet, there have been no hard-and-fast cases of any threat to human health or indeed of the kind of 'genetic pollution' (with genes passing to other species) that campaigners here in Europe have made so much of.

However, this patina of regulatory effectiveness masks substantial deficiencies in the system, with both US agencies having to rely predominantly on research studies carried out by the companies themselves. What goes into these studies and what gets left out is anybody's guess, as they're rarely made available for public scrutiny on the grounds of commercial confidentiality. The industry has also been adept at winning support in the highest echelons of government, not least through a steady exchange of senior staff moving between the biotech industry and the US administration.

Interestingly, America's powerful consumer and environment groups are now beginning to stir, and it's highly unlikely that American biotech companies will have such an easy time of it in the future. In August 1999, one of the biggest American food processors announced that all its suppliers would have to segregate GM from non-GM crops, opening the way for the kind of 'traceability' and proper labelling that US politicians continue to argue are completely unnecessary. Later the same year, the first instances of 'crop trashing' in America were recorded, and a battery of lawsuits filed against both the biotech companies and government regulators.

In the UK (as we saw in Chapters 2 and 3), post-BSE levels of confidence in the government's scientific advisors and regulators have sunk to a very low ebb. So much so that it's become extremely difficult for the UK government even to trial GM crops. Through the summer of 1999, one official trial site after another was trashed by anti-GM campaigners, leading on one high-profile occasion to the arrest of Greenpeace Director Peter Melchett.

Encouraged by surveys that show that nearly one-third of the public is not prepared to wait for the outcome of further trials, demanding that GM crops should be banned outright, the case that Greenpeace makes is a simple one. They assert that we already know as much as we need to know about GM crops, and none of it is good; that trials of this kind are too risky, and that no safeguards (such as buffer zones around the sites) will ever be adequate to prevent widespread 'genetic pollution' wreaking environmental havoc. For Greenpeace, if the Precautionary Principle means anything in practice, it means not even trialling such crops, let alone licensing them for commercial use.

Peter Melchett and I have been involved in environmental campaigning for a very long time. I have a huge amount of respect for him personally, and undying admiration for Greenpeace. But on this occasion I believe he is fundamentally misguided in pursuing a course of action which is anti-scientific, disproportionately and manipulatively emotive, and potentially devastating to the credibility of those seeking to put the Precautionary Principle at the heart of environmental decision-making.

Whichever way you look at it, we need the data that the trials have been set up to produce. And a lot more data beyond that. But if the Precautionary Principle is used not just to constrain risky innovation, but to halt even the gathering of the data on which any rational decision-making process must rest, then it's dead in the political water as a serious policy tool. And with it our claim to be as concerned about 'sound science' as anyone employed by government or big business.

The Genetics Debate

Such concerns provide a very deep backdrop to all the much more exciting stuff going on front of stage. Trust remains the central story line. Every time another politician tells us that we have 'nothing to worry about', or another company scientist trots out the old line that 'there's nothing special about genetic modification: it's just the latest in a long line of selective breeding techniques,' one can almost hear their credibility rating dropping another notch.

True enough, nature has been 'recombining' genes since life on earth began, and we have been shaping our own combinations almost since the start of settled agriculture, by selecting both plants and animals for particular characteristics of benefit to us. While the motivation that underpins genetic engineering is indeed age-old, the technology itself is qualitatively different. Until now, there have been clear limits to our powers: we could not create a new variety that could not theoretically have come about in nature without our intervention.

Today, the 'hard lines' between different organisms and species are beginning to melt away; we can now pick and choose individual genes from one organism to introduce into a totally different and unrelated organism, crossing all biological boundaries, in combinations that nature never could and never would bring together. An 'antifreeze' gene from the Arctic flounder would never, ever find its way into a strawberry. There are few technical limits to these genetic recombinations, and those limits will soon be overcome. Firing alien genes into a different genome is exactly the same thing as introducing exotic species into a foreign eco-system. Moreover, there are profound philosophical implications here, as Jeremy Rifkin points out in his excellent book *The Biotech Century* (1998):

> Living things are no longer perceived as birds and bees, foxes and hens, but as bundles of genetic information. All living beings are drained of their substance and turned into abstract messages. Life becomes a code to be deciphered. There is no longer any question of sacredness or specialness. How could there be, when there are no longer any recognizable boundaries to respect? In the new way of thinking about evolution, structure is abandoned. Nothing exists in the moment. Everything is pure activity, pure process. How can any living thing be deemed sacred when it is just a pattern of information?

This is the very essence of the genetics revolution, and to claim that it's no more than the next natural step in a 3.85-billion-year process of evolution is either disingenuous (with people arguing along the lines of 'well, since we ourselves are part of nature, everything we do, for evolutionary good or ill, must by definition be natural') or deeply dishonest. It's a great deal more than that, and needs to be addressed at that level of heightened significance.

Unfortunately, in both philosophical and regulatory terms, things seem to have been done to date more by sleight of hand than by the kind of measured and open process that a politically mature society should aspire to. That, I am sure, will now change, and it's important to keep a sense of proportion here; surprising though it may sound, these are still very early days in the genetics debate. A wide range of claims concerning the benefits of GM crops have been advanced by biotech companies:

- That they will help reduce applications of pesticides, with lower volumes of carefully targeted chemicals taking over from the indiscriminate use of broad spectrum chemicals.
- That they will increase yields and therefore benefit farmers economically at a time of considerable financial uncertainty.
- That they will help reduce soil erosion as it's easier to grow GM crops without constantly turning the soil as part of a weed-control programme.
- That GM crops will help 'feed the world' as conventional farming techniques run up against constraints on land use and soil fertility.

Each of these claims has been challenged by campaigners in both Europe and the United States, and further concerns raised:

- That substantial amounts of chemicals are still used in GM farming, potentially causing even more damage to a whole host of different species.
- That pollen from GM crops will 'contaminate' non-GM crops, particularly organic crops, making it impossible to offer consumers genuinely GM-free produce.
- That GM crops are just as vulnerable to pests becoming resistant to the pesticides used against them as conventional crops.

- That genes will inevitably be transferred from GM crops to their wild-growing relatives, causing all sorts of problems once they are out and about in the wild.
- That all this has nothing to do with making life better either for consumers or farmers, but everything to do with increasing profitability through increased market share in the global economy.

Over and above environmental concerns, there are some who continue to raise fears about the potential impact of GM crops on human health as well as on the environment. These concerns were explored in detail by Sir Robert May (the UK government's Chief Scientist) and Professor Liam Donaldson (the UK's Chief Medical Officer) in a very helpful report in May 1999. Acknowledging that 'nothing can be absolutely certain in a field of rapid scientific and technological development', it nonetheless points out that there is no evidence at all at the moment of any threat to human health.

And so it will go on, with claim and counter-claim, for many years to come, as the independent scientific data gradually builds up, and as the level of understanding gradually increases. We will come to accept that there are specific issues to be addressed for each GM crop, and that generalizations in this area are usually not helpful. Talking of GM crops as if they were all one and the same (as the media often tends to do) is downright misleading.

But there are a few problems that are generic to almost all GM crop releases. The first is the inevitability that there will be some transfer of genes between GM crops and what are endearingly referred to as their 'weedy wild relatives'. If resistance to a particular herbicide, for instance, is transferred from GM oilseed rape to a wild relative, the weedy variety becomes as resistant as the commercial crop, raising all sorts of questions about downstream environmental impacts and the possible emergence of 'superweeds'. At that stage, there can be no recall to the laboratory.

That this kind of 'horizontal transfer' will happen is no longer disputed, even by the most enthusiastic advocates of GM crops. 'It's obvious that transgenes will get out', according to Geoff Squire from the Scottish Crops Research Institute in Dundee. 'The big question is, does it matter?'

As far as Jeremy Rifkin is concerned, it matters a great deal. His views on genetic pollution are characteristically trenchant:

> Look at the landscape. There will be plants over millions of acres producing biodegradable plastics, chemicals and vaccines, all encoding for specific genes that can jump and fix for herbicide, pesticide and viral resistance in weedy relatives. I don't think you even have to be an alarmist. If just a small fraction of these introductions turn out to be long-term pests, then we have irreversible damage to ecosystems. It could be devastating.
>
> (*The Biotech Century*)

On the other hand, there's some evidence that escaped transgenes of this kind do not in fact fare very well in competition with other plants, and quickly die out. But there's very little independent data one way or the other, which continues to play into the hands of those who want to see potential problems downplayed.

So when Professor Alan Grey (of the UK Institute of Terrestrial Ecology) presented his research on GM oilseed rape to the Advisory Committee on Releases to the Environment (ACRE), indicating that there were indeed some worries about horizontal transfer but that it was impossible to quantify the risk without further research, the Committee instantly decided that the risk was not sufficiently substantial to impose a moratorium! The one and only *bona fide* environmentalist on ACRE at that time (Julie Hill, a former Director of the Green Alliance) publicly dissented from that view:

> I dissented from the original decision to give the go-ahead to this product because of uncertainties about how far the genes would spread into wild species, and what would be the long-term consequences of that spread. The Precautionary Principle suggests that we should do more to understand the long-term impacts before proceeding.

In circumstances like this, the Precautionary Principle must be allowed to come into its own, and given that this whole question of 'genetic pollution' was one of the main issues that prompted English Nature (the UK government's own scientific advisors on conservation issues) to recommend a three-year moratorium on GM crops, you would have thought that the government would have been inclined to listen at the time. But the problem here is not so much scientific as commercial – on both sides of the Atlantic. Both Prime Minister Tony Blair and President Clinton remain almost uncritically committed to the advancement of GM foods and their respective biotech industries. They may occasionally intimate that 'the jury is still out', but they really don't mean it. Precaution here looks like an unacceptable barrier to legitimate business, whatever the scientific warning signals may be.

Interestingly, many ecologists are far more concerned about the problem of resistance than they are about horizontal transfer. As we saw in Chapter 4, fifty years of pest-eradication policies have left us facing one adamantine truth: nature (as in weeds or pests) will almost always outwit man. We can beat them back, get them temporarily under control, limit the damage they cause, but pretty soon they'll have the upper hand all over again, this time with new, resistant staying power!

Companies like Monsanto continue to imply that they will be able to overcome the resistance problem by engineering the chemical agent right into the plants themselves. Again, this is either disingenuous or dishonest. Just as most pests have learned to survive an unremitting blizzard of highly toxic poisons out there in the field, so they will learn to survive the next blizzard of rather more subtle, genetically modified equivalents. From a beetle's perspective, there's not a jot of difference between coping with a poison in the plant or a poison sprayed on to the plant; a few will survive, and their offspring will develop resistance, feeding off crops that are then defenceless.

How long, for instance, will it take the redoubtable Colorado potato beetle to adapt its way through the genetically engineered defences of Monsanto's New Leaf potatoes? Two years? Five years? And then what? The New Leaf Plus Potato with Added (GM) Venom?

Another two years? And then what? A return to even more toxic chemicals?

Though you can understand why the biotech companies are reconciled to such a prospect (endless new products to dangle in front of entrapped farmers and compliant consumers), it is astonishing that serious scientists can be so childishly enthusiastic at the prospect of swapping today's chemical treadmill for tomorrow's genetic treadmill, all in pursuit of the unattainable dream of pest eradication.

Exploring the Alternatives

This issue is of particular concern to the organic movement. For many years, organic farmers have been permitted to use a particular soil bacterium (*Bacillus thuringiensis*, or BT), which is deadly to certain target insects such as caterpillars. Many crops are now being engineered with the gene for the BT toxin built in, and precisely because the BT toxin is being manufactured by the plant all the time (instead of being applied every now and then when dealing with a serious infestation), many insects will inevitably become resistant to it.

The US Environmental Protection Agency reckons that most key insect pests will have developed resistance over the next five years, and have proposed new rules requiring farmers to plant 'reserves' of non-GM equivalent crops (at up to 40 per cent of the total acreage planted) where pests will not be able to build up resistance. The chances of this working are close to zero, leaving organic farmers without their biological weapon of last resort.

We're only just beginning to understand the knock-on effects of insect-resistant crops of this kind. Last year, the Scottish Crop Research Institute published details of an interesting experiment which showed that ladybirds fed on aphids that had themselves been feeding off transgenic, insect-resistant potatoes, laid fewer eggs and lived only half as long as ladybirds feeding on 'normal' aphids.

And in May 1999, scientists at Cornell University startled hitherto laid-back Americans with an elegant experiment involving the much-loved monarch butterfly – sometimes referred to as 'the Bambi of the insect world'. The migratory monarch travels up from Mexico to breed in the mid-West and as far north as Canada, where its caterpillars feed on the leaves of the milkweed plant. Having noticed that milkweed growing near maize crops got covered in maize pollen, Cornell entomologist John Losey sprinkled pollen from Monsanto's BT-maize (which now comprises more than 30 per cent of the US maize crop) on milkweed leaves and fed them to monarch caterpillars. Around half of them died within four days, whereas pollen from unmodified maize had no effect whatsoever on an equivalent control group.

Let's just stand back here for a moment, as the US Office of Technology Assessment did in 1988:

> In the long term (10 to 50 years), unforeseen ecological consequences of using recombinant organisms in agriculture are not only likely, they are probably inevitable. But it is crucial to put this into perspective: it is difficult to describe a critical scenario that will lead to a problem that is different in kind from the problems caused by past agricultural practices.

That may be. But nor does GM offer any sustainable solutions to those problems. Not one of the principal concerns about modern intensive farming (e.g. the dangerous dependence on monocultures, loss of crop diversity, long-term impacts on soil fertility, the persistence of pest-eradication fantasies, knock-on damage to rural communities, particularly in Third World countries, inadequate regulation, the growing concentration of ownership and power within the food industry, etc., etc.) is addressed by the gradual but seemingly inexorable move to GM farming. All we would appear to be getting, on top of all the same old problems, is a host of new problems and new risks.

And that's the nub of it. All the comparisons being made at the moment are between conventional chemical farming and GM farming. Even if you accept that certain GM crops will bring lasting environmental benefits (which most environmentalists currently don't), the comparison between GM farming and organic farming, or other kinds of sustainable agriculture, is at least as important.

Especially in the context of the 'feed the world' debate. The biotech industry asserts that, like it or not, we simply must press on down the GM path as that's the only way we're going to feed the world. As the propaganda for EuropaBio puts it, 'biotechnology is a key factor in the fight against famine.' Monsanto pressed the same button in its 1998 advertising campaign: 'Worrying about starving future generations won't feed them. Food biotechnology will.'

This kind of emotional blackmail really does make my hackles rise – though it's indisputably true that we are facing an enormous challenge. World population will increase from around 6 billion today to 8.25 billion by 2015, and stabilize (if we're lucky) at around 10 billion in the second half of the next century. The amount of new land available for crop production is extremely limited in almost every part of the world. It will indeed be a huge struggle to feed all those new millions, and there are fears that rapid climate change will make that struggle even harder.

But the problem is not the availability of food, as was pointed out in a powerful briefing from a campaigning organization called The Cornerhouse in October 1998:

More than enough food is already being produced to provide everyone in the world with a nutritious and adequate diet – according to the United Nations World Food Programme, one and a half times the amount required. Yet at least one-seventh of the world's people (some 800 million) go hungry. About one-quarter of these are children. They starve because they do not have access to land on which to grow food, or do not have the money to buy food, or do not live in a country with a state welfare system. Genetic engineering and agriculture will do nothing to address these underlying structural causes of hunger. On the contrary, it is likely to do much to exacerbate them.

That's not just a view held by Western elites. Responding to those who have claimed that the campaign to ban GM crops is undermining the position of starving people in countries like Ethiopia, Tewolde Berhan Gebre Egziabher, Ethiopia's negotiator on the Convention on

Biological Diversity, stated in 1998: 'There are still hungry people in Ethiopia, but they are hungry because they have no money, no longer because there is no food to buy. We strongly resent the abuse of our poverty to sway the interests of the European public.'

And what good are today's GM crops to poorer countries? Much of the research done to date has been to meet the needs of food processors and retailers in the developed world rather than the needs of hungry people. 90 per cent of GM soya and 60 per cent of GM maize are grown to feed animals, not humans, and boosting meat production is probably the least effective way of meeting people's food needs. Even some of the newer 'breakthroughs' (to delay ripening or rotting fruits and vegetables, for instance) will be of interest exclusively to commercial producers in poorer southern countries as they seek to export more to richer northern countries. Not much nutritional benefit for hungry people there either.

As far as Third World farmers are concerned, GM crops will almost certainly be more expensive, input costs will rise and genetic diversity will be further eroded. Farms will get bigger, small farmers will be forced off the land, and pretty soon we'll be witnessing a re-run of the huge social and environmental costs caused by the Green Revolution back in the 1960s and 1970s. What's more, once they really get into their swing, our genetic revolutionaries will almost certainly end up doing more harm than good to poorer countries. There's a huge amount of research going on dedicated to finding genetically engineered alternatives to things like cocoa butter (for chocolate), sugar, sweeteners, natural flavourings like vanilla, and oils used in food processing – all of which would cut out Third World suppliers altogether.

Interestingly, the biotech companies have become rather more cautious about making grandiose claims on behalf of the world's starving masses than they were before the debate flared up in Europe. But politicians are still eloquently parroting their 'feed the world' propaganda, and even those who really should know better have unthinkingly bought into the idea of there being some 'moral imperative' in pushing GM for the benefit of Third World farmers – including members of the influential Nuffield Council on Bioethics in the UK, whose otherwise impressive report in June 1999 reached new levels of naïvety and gullibility on this particular issue.

It simply isn't true (as their report indicated) that we've got to 'go for GM anyway' simply because there's no other way of meeting the food needs of all those millions of people. In fact, there's a growing amount of firm evidence demonstrating that there are all sorts of ways of dramatically improving yields using integrated pest management, agroforestry, mixed cropping, lower levels of chemicals and fertilizers and so on. Systematic investment in educating subsistence farmers in disease control and other sustainable techniques is proving to be one of the most cost-effective ways of directly improving the living standards of poorer rural populations.

So there are alternatives, which need to be properly funded. But that's not to say there won't be an important role in the future for certain GM crops which may well prove to be of real benefit to developing countries and to poor, subsistence farmers. Like many people, I am excited by the prospect of drought-resistant crops, of crops that will grow in the kind of saline or heavily mineralized soils that won't sustain normal crops, of crops with enhanced nutritional value like GM rice enriched with iron to help ward off anaemia or with vitamin A to rectify a deficiency, of bananas and sweet potatoes resistant to the kind of viruses or fungal diseases that cause major damage year after year and require the application of huge amounts of chemicals. The same concerns apply here (about potential environmental impacts downstream, for instance), and, however socially benign they may be, all such crops must be tested and monitored as rigorously as any of the current generation of commodity crops, which merely tighten biotech companies corporate grip on the farmer. But to decree *a priori* that work of this kind should not proceed on account of fundamentalist opposition to the use of GM techniques in all circumstances, for all time, does not seem to me either intellectually convincing or ethically acceptable.

As we wrestle with the concept of 'sustainable agriculture' (systems of food production that can be sustained indefinitely over time to meet the needs of a substantially larger human population), there may well prove to be a role for certain GM crops – subject to all the caveats raised in this chapter. The greater the benefits that a GM crop offers, the more open people will be to accepting a certain level of risk. The boundaries between what we now describe as 'organic', 'chemical' or 'GM', are likely to soften; whatever the descriptor, all production systems will be bound by the same discipline of sustainability.

Right now, however, the prospects for GM do not look good. There's growing opposition to GM not just in Europe but in many developing countries. Farmers' organizations in India, for example, find it hard to believe that biotech companies have any real concern for their subsistence farmers when they're simultaneously intent both on stripping their biological assets (by taking out patents on indigenous germ-plasm) and conjuring up new ideas like the much discussed 'terminator technology' or 'suicide seeds'. This technology will allow companies to stop farmers carrying over seeds from one growing season to the next by introducing a gene to render those seeds infertile. Companies argue this is the only way they can protect their 'intellectual property' – i.e. the intellectual investment they have made in new GM crops. Just about everyone else sees such developments as a further attempt by the biotech companies to dominate the entire value chain from seed production all the way through to final product. Under intense pressure from campaigners and its own advisors, Monsanto pledged not to commercialize the 'terminator technology' in October 1999 – whereupon Greenpeace instantly challenged Bob Shapiro to sell the patent for £1. The offer was declined, prompting sceptics to point out that this might be little more than a defensive PR gesture on the part of a humbled Monsanto – and other biotech companies could easily step in to take over the terminator.

This is not a debate that can be moderated, let alone resolved, by the use of science alone. As we saw in Chapter 3, the scientific debate about GM is 'framed' by the social and political context in which new products are being developed and solutions sought to current and future problems. In that context, politicians and scientists need to be a great deal less dismissive of people's anxieties about genetic engineering.

Far from being bamboozled by sensationalist media coverage, it seems more likely to me that people are making quite sophisticated, if intuitive, judgments about relative risks and benefits. The biotech companies have as yet entirely failed to provide a convincing account of the real benefits either for us or for future generations. There's just not enough 'added value' in the move to GM crops to make acceptable what people perceive to be the risks and questionable motives entailed in that move.

Other commercial aspects of the GM debate are now looming ever larger. If American companies and the US administration continue to ride roughshod over European and Third World concerns about GM crops, many people are now predicting that we will see a sequence of trade disputes of so intractable and extreme a nature as to make the 1990s current problems with Caribbean bananas and hormone-treated beef look like a teddy-bears' picnic.

In the UK, it's this extraordinary combination of factors (scientific, commercial, ethical, philosophical, political) that makes genetic modification this government's sternest test of its use of science in policy making. The decisions it takes in this area will colour everything else it does on the broader terrain of sustainable development.

CHAPTER 7

THE SCIENCE OF SUSTAINABILITY

The preceding chapters have looked at three very different sets of issues: toxics and micro-pollutants; climate change; genetic engineering. All scientifically complex, with a lot of 'grey' between the usual extremes of black and white. All politically controversial, with an abundance of elephant traps and potential media and voter sensitivities.

Environmentalists understandably (and justifiably) complain that politicians devote too little time to sustainability issues. But when you step back and ask why, it's not so surprising. They're difficult, and require a lot of time, which politicians have very little of. They're contested, and require a certain amount of scientific literacy, which politicians seem to have even less of. They're as much about the future as the present, with fewer votes to be had out of them than even the most courageous and future-oriented of politicians might feel comfortable with.

But we're still making much heavier going of getting to grips with these and many other environmental issues than seems justified. I believe that there is a reason for this, and this resides in the way that we use (and abuse) science today, and in the obvious inadequacies of conventional scientific methodologies and philosophical tenets. It's that hypothesis I shall be putting to the test again in this chapter.

At my first ever Ecology Party Conference in 1974 (long before it became the Green Party), I remember Edward Goldsmith fulminating against 'the blinkered reductionism of the UK science establishment' – blinkered in the same way as a racehorse is, in order to focus attention on the winning post ahead, minimizing the possibility of being diverted by stuff going on to the left or to the right. 'Scientists are so obsessed with all the little details downstream that they've forgotten the systems from which they derive upstream.'

Twenty-five years on, that's as true today as it was then. Environmental science is almost exclusively geared to measuring, managing and mitigating downstream environmental impacts caused by our industrial way of life. To be sure, we're getting better at analysing and (eventually) dealing with these downstream 'pollution problems', but in ways that often produce no net or lasting benefit. No sooner is one problem 'solved' than another looms up to take its place. Rival scientists slug it out with conflicting interpretations of the 'facts', accusing each other of bad science, even as the 'facts' are constantly changing around them as our knowledge grows.

Our ignorance about many of these downstream impacts is still overwhelming. As toxicologists have been pointing out for years, we don't even know how many of the chemicals used in Western society cause cancer. Grotesquely inadequate testing and authorization procedures in the '50s and '60s, in both the United States and Europe, means that we are now having to carry out hugely expensive retrospective tests, often involving extensive animal experiments.

Writing in 1997, Sandra Steingraber gave some idea of the scale of the problem:

> Researchers have estimated that of the 75,000 chemicals now in commercial use, somewhat fewer than 5 to 10 per cent of these might reasonably be considered carcinogenic in humans. Five to 10 per cent means 3750 to 7500 different chemicals. The number of substances we have identified and regulate as carcinogens is, at present, less than 200.

'Proper scientific methods' demand that each and every one of the thousands of potential carcinogens must be individually identified, tested, re-tested and finally appraised for the degree of risk entailed in its use in agriculture or pest control. Anyone claiming some 'probable' or 'possible' cause-and-effect linkage simply by looking at the statistics will be instantly arraigned on the charge of 'ecological fallacy'. Causative relationships must be proved beyond reasonable doubt; no chemical will be found guilty of causing harm until a full complement of victims has been properly accounted for.

Such is the mighty science of toxicology, developed to test risk exposure to individual toxic chemicals in laboratory conditions. Such an approach is almost entirely incapable of testing for synergistic (combined) effects of two or more chemicals, or testing for effects out there in the big wide world, or testing for cumulative effects over many years. As cancer expert Ross Hume Hall says:

> In the open world, each of us – babies, toddlers, young people, old people – carries hundreds, if not thousands, of different chemical residues from pesticides, industrial chemicals and food additives in our bodies. Toxicology is blind to the dangers of carrying this lifetime burden, a blindness which clearly works in favour of the chemical industry.

Yet the chemical industry has made sure that environmental regulations are written in such a way that the burden of proof rests on the regulator to prove each individual chemical, in isolation, is harmful. It is a deeply politicized process, with big companies often calling the shots with the politicians, who then compel their regulatory agencies to fritter away untold sums of money 'messing around downstream' when it's abundantly obvious that the focus should be upstream. To call this 'good science' is absurd.

It's interesting to compare such flawed procedures with the visionary and highly effective approach of our prototype public health agencies in the nineteenth century, which forced municipal authorities to install basic drainage, sewerage and clean water systems long before the specific causative links between contaminated drinking water and diseases like cholera were 'proved'. It may sound odd, but when considering the proper and responsible use of science in the public interest, some argue that we're worse off now than our nineteenth-century forebears.

The Laws of Thermodynamics

With our regulators conveniently ensnared downstream, and often debarred from commenting on systems upstream, our politicians continue to interpret all these environmental problems as a series of single-issue malfunctions in a basically sound wealth-creation system. But they aren't. They are symptoms of an inherently dysfunctional system, and it's dysfunctional because it systematically ignores some of the most fundamental scientific principles on which our understanding of life on Earth rests. These are the laws of thermo-dynamics, or more properly, the laws of conservation of energy and matter.

Readers may be inclined to skip this section for greener pastures ahead. But please don't: it's precisely because we've so often skipped the thinking that lies behind the laws of thermodynamics, in our con-stant and impatient pursuit of material progress, that we've ended up with a system that just isn't working any more.

Energy exists in all sorts of different forms (heat, light, motion, etc.), which are constantly being transformed from one into another. It's these transformations that power our economy and enable us to carry out useful work. The first law of thermodynamics simply states that energy is neither created nor destroyed during these transforma-tions. To use Tim Jackson's explanation in *Material Concerns*, 1996 (by far the most helpful book in this area that I've encountered):

> The total energy input always matches the total energy output. For example, when coal is burned, chemical energy is transformed into thermal energy. But the heat output is no more and no less than the energy stored in the chemical bonds of the coal to start with. What's more, the total mass of the material inputs to a transformation process is equal to the total mass of the material outputs.

If the first law of thermodynamics states that the amount of energy remains constant during transformation, the second law of thermo-dynamics states that the availability of that energy to perform useful work becomes less and less as it passes through successive trans-formations.

These laws lead to a simple but all-important conclusion: nothing ever disappears. Every atom in the universe today has been part of the universe since the big bang, and will continue to be part of the universe until the end of time. Everything has to go somewhere, and 'stuff' has a way of spreading. And every time energy and matter are converted into another form, their quality is degraded and they become less useful to us.

We know all this from our own daily experience. Natural resources that are extracted or harvested to power our economy must eventually return to nature. Steel eventually rusts, fossil fuels are burned, wood rots, carpets turn to dust – not the other way round. And the value of these resources (and the products in which we incorporate them) is directly related to their order, by which we mean the quality or concentration of energy and matter. As that concentration is dispersed, its value drops.

In that respect, it's not things or molecules that we're consuming, but the order inherent in them. When we burn a gallon of petrol in an internal combustion engine, we do not really consume those hydrocarbons, but benefit from the work they perform as they are being transformed. When we drink water, we are not only consuming it physically, but also consuming its quality in terms of the concentration of clean molecules. It's that which has value. It is the availability and maintenance of this quality that determines the prosperity of human kind, and if society consumes quality more quickly than it can be reconstituted through natural systems, then we are in effect becoming poorer not richer.

So where does that quality come from? The American eco-entrepreneur, Paul Hawken, puts it as follows:

Contrary to what many people might believe, the rate and capacity of the Earth to create material quality depends not on human-driven activities, but on the sun. Virtually all our human activities remove or consume quality. As ingenious and important as industrial practices are, they also use up quality and order. Nature has the capacity to recycle wastes and reconstitute them into new resources of concentrated material quality. However, its capacity is regulated by sunlight and photosynthesis, not by economic theory or politics. Today's extraction and processing of resources is overwhelming that capacity, while the waste from these processes systematically builds up in our water, air, soil, wildlife – and in ourselves.

At one level, this is all well understood by scientists, whatever their specialized discipline may be. But it's not an active understanding. The reason we're in such an ecological pickle today is that we have wittingly and systematically ignored those laws throughout the Industrial Revolution. We have assumed that the human species is somehow not bound by them. Out of sight, out of mind; dilute and disperse; mine it, make it, chuck it; bury or burn: these have been the literal watchwords of a wealth-creating machine that to this day has never paid the real costs for its use of the Earth's resources.

As many have pointed out, the very term 'waste disposal' is an illusion. People somehow assume that petrol disappears when it is burned, or that rubbish no longer exists when it's incinerated. But neither is the case. Waste can change its form, but it cannot be thrown away because the Earth is a closed system with respect to matter. There is no 'away'. Politicians and regulators have connived in that illusion – and continue to do so. Scientists and engineers have buttoned their lip, and crossed their fingers that the reckoning wouldn't come in their own day. For they know with absolute certainty that one day it will come. That's what the laws of thermodynamics tell us. Everything has to go somewhere. Nothing disappears. These are not just interesting hypotheses or bright ideas. They are laws – like the law of gravity – which cannot be ignored or avoided.

It's important to put these laws in their proper evolutionary context. Life has been unfolding on this planet for roughly 3.5 billion years. For much of that time, it consisted of countless zillions of bacteria gradually cleaning up all the poisonous gases, radio-nuclides and heavy metals in the atmosphere that made life as we know it today wholly impossible. Over many hundreds of millions of years, those 'nasties' were detoxified and safely sequestered away through the slow process of biomineralization in the surface of the Earth, until it eventually became possible for 'higher', more complex life forms to emerge.

From then on, the complexity and diversity of life forms on Earth gradually increased, notwithstanding a number of cataclysmic 'extinction spasms' which destroyed most life forms present during those periods. But each time diversity built back up again, so that biologists now calculate there are more species on planet Earth than there have ever been before. And no doubt it would build back up again even if (in the most apocalyptic of eco-scenarios) we manage to wipe out millions of species in the process of wiping out our own.

Those who talk therefore of 'the human species destroying life on Earth' are clearly guilty of hyperbole. But that doesn't mean (as has often been argued) that proponents of such views are reconciled to continuing environmental devastation (in our terms) on account of the fact that (in evolutionary terms) it's little more than a passing pinprick. Even if you strip away the fantasies of us being in control, and the arrogance of those who suppose that the unique purpose of 3.5 billion years of evolution was to produce the human species, it seems only human in evolutionary terms to want to improve things for our own species by protecting the life-support systems on which we and every other species depend.

And that's where you begin to wonder just how much more insane things can get. As is now universally acknowledged, the sustainability of humankind (that is, our capacity for continuance as a species) depends on the sustainability of countless other species and on the relative stability of those life-support systems that sustain those species and maintain planetary balance. But imagine, for one surreal moment, that you were an alien sent down to Earth with a simple mission: to assess how to destabilize life on Earth as rapidly and comprehensively as possible with a view to getting rid of humankind and making Earth available for subsequent colonization by inhabitants of your own planet. Having read up on your thermodynamics and systems biology, and taken a careful look at what was going on, it wouldn't take you long to send back the following report to your eager Commander-in-Chief:

Dear Boss,

Destabilizing life on Earth could be much easier than we thought. All we have to do is:

1 Persuade the human species to dig up and mine as much of the surface area of the Earth as possible, ostensibly to extract oil and gas, minerals, precious metals and so on, but in reality to spew back out into the atmosphere a substantial proportion of all those toxic elements it took 3.5 billion years to lock away safely in the crust of the Earth.

2 Persuade the human species to use its limited intelligence to manufacture as many synthetic compounds as possible which Nature has no way of absorbing or gradually breaking down. Persuade them that true happiness lies exclusively in the purchase of things made in this way, and that all the toxic waste gradually building up in Nature is a price worth paying for progress.

3 Persuade the human species to multiply at a rate over and above natural replacement (ie for each couple to have more than an average of 2.1 children), and to cover over as much as possible of the green surfaces of the Earth with houses, roads, factories, offices, recreation centres, Millennium Domes and so on, in the process undermining Nature's ability to put the order back into the thermodynamic mess these humans are creating.

4 Persuade the leaders of the human species that it makes a lot of sense for the rich to go on getting richer and the poor to go on getting poorer, and that there's no alternative to this anyway as that's what the religion of their so-called 'free market' dictates.

P.S. We won't need to marshal any invading force to put this war plan into action, as these very helpful human beings are already hard at work on all four action points without any encouragement from ourselves. Another few decades, and the job will be done.

Yours in Earth-bound obedience . . . .

The Natural Step

There's a serious intent behind this frivolity. To understand what sustainability means, it's necessary first to understand what unsustainability means in terms of first-order scientific principles. If something is genuinely sustainable, it means it will go on more or less indefinitely; if it's unsustainable, it means it won't. Simple as that.

And that's where an initiative called The Natural Step comes in. Developed by an eminent Swedish cancer scientist, Karl-Henrik Robèrt, it defines and explains sustainability in terms of four 'system conditions' – conditions that we must meet as soon as possible if we want to continue living sustainably on planet Earth.

System Condition 1
Substances from the Earth's crust must not systematically increase in nature. This means that fossil fuels, metals and other materials are not extracted at a faster rate than their slow redeposit into the Earth's crust.

System Condition 2
Substances produced by society must not systematically increase in nature. This means that man-made substances are not produced at a faster pace than they can be broken down by nature.

System Condition 3
The physical basis for the productivity and diversity of nature must not be systematically diminished. This means that the nature's 'green spaces' are not diminished in quality, and renewable resources are only harvested at rates that ensure constant natural regeneration.

System Condition 4
We must be fair and efficient in meeting basic human needs. This means in the sustainable society that basic human needs must be met with the most resource-efficient methods possible, including a just resource distribution.

These 'sustainability conditions' correspond to the four mechanisms for destabilizing life on Earth alluded to before, and were arrived at by a quite remarkable consensus-building process in Sweden in the 1980s. Robèrt's initial impulse was to carve through the usual downstream scientific bickering that dominated the environment debate in Sweden at that time, to rework the laws of thermodynamics and the basic principles of cell biology (the cells of plants, animals and humans share a similar structure and have the same fundamental requirements in order to sustain life), and to distil all that into a framework that could then be used by businesses, politicians, educationalists and so on. Drawing in a group of top scientists, he challenged them not to just go on disagreeing with what he was proposing, but to help him improve it. Twenty-one versions later, a consensus statement emerged, from which the four System Conditions were subsequently derived.

The great strength of The Natural Step lies in these scientific foundations. After the best part of fifteen years of intensive engagement by a host of different players in a vast array of environmental issues and processes, it's a pretty chaotic scene out there. No common language or mode of scientific discourse exists; there's no shared framework to analyse things on a systematic level. Different standards and approaches compete against each other. Some swear by the techniques of Life Cycle Assessment, whilst others see it as a crude substitute for sound judgment. Ecological 'footprints' and 'rucksacks' line up side by side with MIPS (mass intensity per unit of service) and mass-balance input-output models. They all have something to offer, but to be really useful in these troubled times, where experts on one side of the debate are often locked in battle with experts on the other side, there has to be a way of evolving a shared, science-based mindset to facilitate complex decision-making.

Take the debate about persistent, bio-accumulative toxic materials – those that build up in the tissue of organisms as they get more and more concentrated higher up the food chain. While most European countries are still trying to regulate these materials on a substance-by-substance, toxicological basis, Sweden has upped the ante by declaring that all products sold in Sweden by 2007 should 'be free from substances that are persistent and liable to bioaccumulate'.

This powerful manifestation of The Natural Step's second System Condition has created quite a stir in Sweden and beyond. On the one hand, the Swedish Environment Ministry asserts: 'If a compound is persistent, it may be too late to stop it from doing harm if at some time in the future we discover it is toxic. It is better to stop such things being released at all.'

On the other hand, the Association of Swedish Chemical Industries claims it is 'like banning all cars because you have not done a risk assessment to find out which one is the most dangerous.' An exchange which neatly encapsulates the utter inadequacy of reductionist scientific methodologies struggling to manage 'the downstream impacts', while all the time we should be focusing on the big picture upstream.

What's more, it's not just a build-up of toxic chemicals that can do the damage. Non-toxic 'molecular junk' of every conceivable kind can still destabilize natural systems. According to a report in 1997 from the Ecological Society of America, for instance, human activity has doubled the amount of fixed nitrogen circulating in the planet's eco-systems. So what, most scientists might be tempted to say? Three-quarters of the atmosphere consists of nitrogen anyway, and all organisms require nitrogen to live. But through the use of nitrogen-rich fertilizers, burning fossil fuels, draining wetlands and destroying forests and grasslands, we've now doubled the amount of nitrogen that is available to be 'fixed' by organisms – with increasingly serious consequences. Nitrogen saturation causes toxic algal blooms, urban smogs, the leaching-out of nutrients from soils, tree die-back, and so on. System Conditions One and Three breached in every particular!

Astonishingly, notwithstanding the growing concern about today's environmental problems, it is very rare that scientists, politicians or business people take time out to conceptualize what real sustainability would look like for a company, a scientific research institute, a local authority, an ordinary household, a region, and so on. Though the specifics will vary enormously, the general outline is quite clear. In such a world, our activities would not be dependent on the use of fossil fuels or minerals which exceeded the Earth's natural capacity; we would not be producing chemical compounds or synthetic materials in a manner or quantity deleterious to natural systems (including our own); and our wealth-creating processes would not result in the net depletion of Nature's life-giving and order-restoring resources. Paul Hawken again:

> We have failed to recognize that, just as in the lives of cells, the conditions of ecological systems are not established by human laws but by Nature's rules, rules which are non-negotiable and fundamentally rooted in the laws of physics. This means our research must shift away from the specific effects of environmental deterioration and expand towards the dynamic relationship between societal metabolism and ecological limits. In order to do this, we have to employ a method of understanding rooted in scientific principles that are universally accepted.

That's why it's so irritating when people go on about sustainability being an elusive, 'soft' concept, incapable of adequate definition. Sustainability is just about as hard-edged, uncompromising, quantifiable and scientifically rigorous a concept as exists in the indeterminate world of contemporary policy-making. More to the point, policy-makers and regulators would seem not to want that degree of rigour, as it leaves them far less scope for prevarication on the basis of 'inadequate data', and far less room for creative rhetoric and endless weasel words about trade-offs and the need to balance environmental, social and economic interests. As a result, levels of confusion and background noise continue to rise all the time, as has now been recognized by the Environment Agency in the UK which has supported the development of The Natural Step since its inception as one way of helping to resolve that confusion.

Which takes us directly into the zone of sustainable development – a very different beast from sustainability, although the two are used synonymously even by people who should know better. Sustainable development is a process, not a scientifically definable capacity; it describes the journey we must undertake to arrive at the destination, which is of course sustainability itself; it is essentially driven by political and economic processes, not by science and empirical data; and it can be defined in such a way as to mean almost anything that anybody wants it to mean, which sustainability cannot.

This almost infinite malleability has been hugely beneficial since the concept of sustainable development first appeared in popular political discourse with the publication of the Brundtland Report back in 1987. Instead of triggering instant denial and opposition, 'its protean, open-ended character' has drawn people of every persuasion into the debate. But as Robin Grove-White has pointed out, this open-endedness is now also its greatest vulnerability:

> On present trends, any foreseeable British political regime over the next few years seems likely to be dominated by a strongly economistic conception of the public good, as the imperatives of international competitiveness and control of public expenditure continue to intensify. This being the case, there will be relentless pressure within and outside government to conceive of 'sustainable development' in terms consistent with these imperatives. British industry, in particular, will be concerned to ensure its prospects are hampered by 'sustainability commitments' only to the extent that any constraints are shared by competitors elsewhere.

Farewell sustainability; hello something that might best be described as marginally less unsustainable development. Depressingly, the size of the gap between the two will be determined principally by the speed with which feedback loops in our collapsing life-support systems finally give politicians the kind of incontrovertible evidence they apparently still need. Only then will they begin to legislate for the far more profound changes necessary for genuine sustainability.

CHAPTER 8

THE POLITICS OF ENVIRONMENTAL SCIENCE

If politicians and officials had a rather more focused notion of what sustainability's all about, scientifically, then they might find it easier to shed more light on the many murky and controversial areas they have to deal with.

To be fair, things are getting better. It was once an almost automatic reaction on the part of government to deny that anything untoward was going on and to defend the existing line. We see far less of that these days. However, it's still somewhat surprising how often politicians seem to be caught on the hop, at which point older instincts kick in.

One such is the automatic tendency to blame the media. The UK's GM 'panic' in 1999 provides an absolute classic of its kind. There's no doubt, looking back over the coverage, that the media were in one of their periodic feeding frenzies, the like of which we hadn't seen since the Brent Spar frenzy in 1997. Even Sir Robert May, the government's Chief Scientist, who understands the media well and has seen such episodes a hundred times before, declared himself to be outraged at the sensationalism and sheer ignorance of much of the coverage.

But these things don't happen in a vacuum. The British government had already primed the media's distrust with its rejection of English Nature's advice; its delay in setting up the Food Standards Agency; its almost total misunderstanding of the public mood; its failure to learn any lessons from the BSE crisis, with ministers contradicting each other, clearly confused and resorting to contemptuous dismissal of the views of others; the apparent suppression of a key report from the government itself; a refusal to acknowledge any inadequacies in the UK regulatory system; suspicions of big-business skulduggery, with top-level meetings between ministers and key biotech companies; a Science Minister who couldn't attend key meetings because of his own commercial interests in biotech – and so on and on! If Alastair Campbell, the Prime Minister's Press Officer, had sat down in February 1998 and asked himself how best to engineer a media furore on GM foods a year later, he couldn't possibly have scripted it better.

That is not to absolve the media, especially when it comes to weeding out the 'off-the-wall' stuff. Nor does it absolve environmental organizations, for it's true, historically, that environmentalists have often succeeded in wringing more 'bad news' out of a story, with more sensationalist overtones, than the literally interpreted facts have always warranted. On occasions (Brent Spar being one of them), elements of the media have been complicit in talking up the story, precisely to ensure that it really is 'a story' in their terms. This is particularly true when there are some good visuals to work with, as it's 'the pics that carry the day'. In December 1997, post-Brent Spar, the BBC series *Scare Stories* was highly critical both of environmental organizations and some of the media for their alleged lack of scientific accuracy, let alone balance.

Almost every environmental organization would have to own up to the occasional creative exaggeration of the facts. But it's only in the last decade or so that environmentalists have been listened to at all; before that, they needed a lot of story to get anyone's attention. Even now, it's sometimes necessary to make more of one particular aspect of a story than may be strictly justified in order to get the issue as a whole taken up in the media.

Take Professor Pusztai's notorious potatoes. His experiments on feeding GM potatoes to rats, and his interpretation of the results (controversially indicating that there would be a possible threat to human health from ingesting such potatoes) became the most important element in the 1999 media furore about GM foods in the UK. As most people would now recognize, this was just one experiment among many, no more and no less significant or worrying than literally dozens going on in UK labs right now. But for reasons that had little to do with the experiment itself, this was the one that snagged the media's tripwire. And from that point on, anti-GM campaigners milked it for all it was worth.

Some (including Sir Robert May) would argue that such deliberate imbalance was unethical. Others would argue that such tactics were wholly justified given the relative indifference of the political and scientific establishment to the breakneck development of the GM industry. In the same way that concern about environmental issues is often a surrogate for much deeper but less coherent concerns about our whole industrial way of life, I would argue that Professor Pusztai's GM potatoes were simply a convenient front for a whole host of much more profound ethical and environmental anxieties about the genetics revolution.

So much of this comes back to trust. Back in 1998, postponing the establishment of the Food Standards Agency – or even shelving it altogether, which was seriously considered by ministers despite it having been a key item in Labour's election manifesto – may have looked like a reasonably low-risk, uncontroversial thing to do. But with 9.5 million people in the UK (one in every six of us) suffering from food poisoning or stomach bugs every year, critics were beginning to wonder just how many fatal *E. coli* outbreaks it would take to persuade the government that this really was a priority.

By the same token, not carrying out a root-and-branch review of all the different committees involved in regulating GM foods may have made sense from a cautious, 'if it ain't broke, don't fix it' point of view. But it proved a PR disaster in terms of further eroding the trust in the judgment of these committees – especially given their very heavy industry bias.

As we saw in Chapter 3, there's still a rump of influential scientific opinion that would like to see the whole area of risk management and communication 'totally de-politicized', as if there were some notionally independent and autonomous body to whom the government could hand over responsibility for complex, risk-based issues, just as Chancellor of the Exchequer Gordon Brown handed over responsibility for setting interest rates to the Bank of England. A crazy notion if ever there was one.

Hopefully, in the wake of the BSE crisis and the 1999 GM frenzy, the government will now steer in exactly the opposite direction, and begin to take seriously the need for a much more inclusive way of addressing scientific issues so as to rebuild trust, ensure wider representation in key decision-making processes, and wherever possible, develop consensus positions on controversial issues.

Civic Science

In his book *Environmental Science for Environmental Management* (1999), Tim O'Riordan has advanced some additional requirements on which genuinely inclusive scientific processes will depend: a readiness on the part of politicians to 'let go' by bringing more people into decision-making structures; foregoing the habit of using people as so much 'consultation fodder' in processes that are in reality predetermined and not genuinely open to external inputs; a readiness on the part of participants first to listen (really listen!) and then to reach substantive agreements rather than endlessly grandstand their own prejudices; the necessity to make all regulatory and executive bodies fully transparent, and to ensure that they operate independently of government and are seen to operate independently of government.

We've been very unadventurous in the UK in trying out more participative and inclusive processes; if anything, the centralization of power in the hands of scientific and technical elites would seem to be increasing. Apart from one major consensus conference (the UK National Consensus Conference on Plant Biotechnology, funded by the Biotechnology and Biological Research Council) and a few smaller events (including a fascinating Citizens' Foresight exercise involving a panel of 12 citizens of Brighton exploring the future of agriculture), nothing like enough has been done to try out a wide range of approaches used in other policy areas and in other countries.

It simply isn't possible to think of science any longer as a set of detached processes producing value-free, objective advice for grateful policy-makers to go away and act on. Time after time, the 1998 Royal Commission report emphasizes the importance of this shift, endorsing the idea of more inclusive processes and recommending that government departments and agencies adopt such techniques wherever the issues are 'complex and broad in scope'.

In that vein, it's encouraging that the UK's Department of Trade and Industry saw fit to launch its own Public Consultation on the Biosciences in November 1998, coordinated by the Office of Science and Technology. Its stated aim is to 'explore the wider (including ethical) implications of recent developments in the biosciences', with the field-work being conducted by MORI using a number of citizens' juries and a detailed survey of 1000 people drawn from the People's Panel set up by the Cabinet Office in 1998.

The term 'civic science' was coined by Kai Lee back in 1994 to try and capture some of these developments, and to emphasize the rather obvious reality that science has to be an interactive process between experts and non-experts, based on trust and mutual respect. But many scientists (particularly those who believe in the inviola-bility of the conventional scientific method) remain deeply suspicious of the corrupting influences of normative thinking and emotional subjectivism.

A disproportionate number of these die-hard sceptics have been involved over the years in the UK Committee for the Public Understanding of Science (COPUS), established by the Royal Society back in 1986. As far as one can make out, 'public understanding' to COPUS has meant two things: first, understanding the central reality that the general public is ignorant and therefore prey to a whole host of suspicious influences that are filling their heads with unscientifc and anti-scientific rubbish; second that what really matters is filling those same heads with scientifically authoritative material to set them on the straight and narrow. This is the so-called 'deficit model': people are just ignorant and gullible, and all they need is educating.

That doesn't mean that COPUS hasn't done a lot of useful work. It spends around £500,000 a year in promoting debate and discussion, running a small grants scheme to support innovative developments in public understanding, publishing 'best practice' case studies and guides, and backing the excellent Rhône-Poulenc Prizes for Science Books. But so much of it is done in this lofty, patrician way, with things handed down from them to us; there seems to be little awareness that part of the problem could reside in the model of science that they're trying to promote, and in the overall approach of those trying to promote it.

Back in 1997, Lewis Wolpert (the former Chair of COPUS) and the British geneticist Steve Jones stirred up a real hornets' nest when they suggested that it wasn't just the general public that needed corrective in-filling education, but any intellectual who didn't have a formal scientific training. This represented the crudest of attempts not just to reassert C.P. Snow's 'two cultures' theory, but to make out that scientists (in terms of the way they think) are a race apart. And a superior race at that. With tongue firmly in cheek, science author Ralph Levinson has pointed out that scientists have got to understand people if they want people to understand science:

> Today we face many problems concerning the food and drink so vital to our well-being, and other important areas of science policy. So SUP, Scientists Understanding People, would be far more useful than PUS (Public Understanding of Science). 'SUP' is a verb, proactive and more wholesome, associated with imbibing tasty substances. But before SUP, could we not have Scientists Learning to Understand the Responses of People, SLURP?

Interestingly enough, the March 1999 COPUS website included reference to a brand-new project, 'Understanding the Public', so perhaps the message is finally getting through!

However deficient the deficit model might be as an overall framework for promoting the public understanding of science, it cannot be denied that there are a number of gaps that certainly need to be filled. And this places a very special responsibility on education systems the world over. Contrary to what you might imagine if you listen to the deficit-gap protagonists, in Britain at least, things have improved considerably over the last twenty years or so. Back in the 1950s, science was taught only to a minority of children – the most academically able at secondary level. Today, science is a National Curriculum

Foundation subject, compulsory for all students up to the age of sixteen, occupying for most about 20 per cent of class time.

It's not, of course, a question of quantity, but of quality. Here, opinions are divided. Some argue that too much time is spent on delivering the facts and filling children with 'content', and not enough on more creative, experiential processes which would enable children to internalize the reality of the way the world works in a far more direct and lasting manner. Predictably, others argue exactly the opposite.

I suspect I'm somewhat biased. My own science education was predominantly content-based, without so much of a sniff of the hands-on beyond crystals and test tubes and things that smelled of rotten cabbages. As a teacher in the 1970s, working closely with science colleagues on environmental issues, it was already much better; and today it's quite different. There's even a move at secondary level to break down some of the time-honoured barriers between the different disciplines of chemistry, physics, biology and geography, with more integrated and modular classes.

What's more, courtesy of organizations like the World Wide Fund for Nature (WWF), the Sierra Club and the Royal Society for the Protection of Birds (RSPB), there is now a wondrous flow of the most exciting and professionally produced educational materials covering every environmental issue under the sun. The vast majority of environmental organizations today are serious about environmental science, avoiding the kind of loose propaganda for which they are occasionally lambasted in the media, and seeking to keep that fine balance between 'speaking truth' and lapsing into partisan special pleading. WWF has to be singled out for particular praise here by pushing out beyond the basics of environmental education into the much more complex terrain of 'education for sustainability', emphasizing linkages between separate subjects and issues, and between ourselves and the rest of the natural world.

At its best, this is a fantastic resource. From the earliest age, through to the end of their formal schooling, children the world over need to understand and experience the depth of that interconnectedness. For many city children in particular, this is indeed a 'deficit' that can only be filled through their teachers and schools. Undoing the psychic damage of more than two hundred years of mis-education (in the West), premised on the separateness of humankind from the rest of life on Earth, is a compelling part of the challenge facing science teachers today.

But how many children are really given access to these insights? Even good 'environmental education' schools can be pretty pedestrian in their approach. Over the years I've become increasingly intrigued by the theory that one of the principal reasons (if not the principal reason) why so many people in the developed world are unhappy, unfulfilled and generally out of sorts is that they are 'alienated' (in the literal sense of the word) from the rest of life on Earth. Ted Roszak has written about this most powerfully in his book *The Voice of the Earth* (1992):

> A culture that can do so much to damage the planetary fabric that sustains it, and yet continues along its course unimpeded, is mad with the madness of a deadly compulsion that reaches beyond our own kind to all the brute innocence about us. We are pressing forward to create a monocultural world-society in which whatever survives must do so as the adjunct of urban-industrial civilization. And the loss that comes of that crime falls upon us as much as any species of plant or animal we annihilate; for the planet will, of course, endure, perhaps to generate new adventures in life in the aeons to come. But we are being diminished by our destructive insensitivity in ways that cripple our ability to enjoy, grow, create. By becoming so aggressively and masterfully 'human', we lose our essential humanity.

Our 'essential humanity' is necessarily Earth-bound, contextualized both physically and cosmologically by the evolution of life on Earth and our part in it. Despite our every effort, we cannot disconnect from that context. The great biologist, E.O. Wilson, suggests in *Biophilia* (1984) that 'the urge to affiliate with other forms of life is to some degree innate', and ascribes all sorts of basic behaviours (gardening, keeping pets, rambling, watching natural history programmes on television, and so on) to a genetic, Earth-loving inheritance that we can ignore but never suppress. In that context, it's fascinating to see how pundits of every political description who regularly ascribe violence and ruthless self-interest (particularly among men) to our genetic inheritance, look askance at those who suggest that other symptoms of psychological unease, alienation and destructive behaviour in our 'denatured' world might be ascribed to that self-same genetic inheritance.

Deeper Anxieties

Of what concern might all this be to the harassed policy-makers and scientists wrestling to make sense of what now looks like an unstoppable flow of environmental controversies? Sort out one, and the next looms up as an instant substitute, larger and even more intractable than the one before. At the moment, for lack of any deeper understanding, each and every one of those controversies is treated as just another symptom of a malfunctioning economy, resulting in another biophysical pressure point, requiring another technological solution.

But it's not as simple as that. We find ourselves in the throes of a worsening environmental crisis not just because of the external reality (more and more people consuming more and more on a finite planet really does result in progressive ecological breakdown), but because of an altogether more subtle internal reality. Is it not probable (as I've suggested before) that people's fears and anxieties about the environment function at many different levels, but are in essence the surface manifestation of a much deeper set of fears and anxieties about the modern industrial world in general?

Again, it's Robin Grove-White who provides this insight in his 1997 article in *The Political Quarterly*:

> The rise of popular environmentalism since the early 1970s has indeed
> reflected a mounting concern about the immense physical 'externalities'
> of advanced industrial societies. But, quite as significantly, it has also
> reflected an anxious and groping reaction against embedded dominant
> patterns of thought and value which underpin these problems. A crucial

element in the increasing effectiveness of environmental NGOs in the 1970s and 1980s was their developing ability to identify and promote issues that would resonate within the mainstream political culture (including, crucially, the media), not only as physically damaging or dangerous, but also as offering symbolic echoes of these wider cultural tensions.

Now that really does make it problematic for the politicians! Even were they able to reform all the regulatory bodies dealing with environmental and health issues, to ensure genuine transparency in scientific decision-making processes, and to energize a new kind of participative 'civic science', they would still find themselves having to deal with a much deeper psychic angst which no amount of good process or 'sound science' would be able to ease away.

Problematic, but hardly surprising. Here we are, at the dawn of a new age of genetics and the biosciences. Book after book, article after article, ministerial speech after ministerial speech positively glows with a sense of pioneering excitement at pushing back the frontiers of science in such breathtakingly brilliant ways. We are all invited to share in that excitement – and in truth, as I've said, it's impossible not to. Whatever else the science of genetics may in due course tell us, it's in our genes (as it's always been) to want to extend those frontiers; hence our admiration for the men and women who take on that challenge.

But we also know (this time from our much more recent history as a species) that there will be a dark side to all this. Something will go badly wrong. There will be a heavy price to pay. Now that it's out of its bottle, the genetic genie has tricks up its sleeve which few at the moment can even begin to discern.

As a child of the 1960s and 1970s, the nuclear genie still looms large for me as a powerful analogy. At Friends of the Earth, I studied in some depth the origins and early days of the nuclear industry, a history filled with brilliant scientists who cared deeply about human-kind and were intensely proud of the 'incalculable benefits' that their new technology would bring. Or so they thought. Potential downstream costs and liabilities were rarely raised, and when they were, promptly dismissed as unsubstantiated scaremongering. But take a long hard look at that nuclear genie lurking in the ruins of Chernobyl, in the psychological aftermath of Three Mile Island, in the terrifying illegal trade in enriched uranium and plutonium that causes security services around the world more sleepless nights than any other single threat to our wellbeing.

For now, that is. Ask yourself: what will be causing them their sleepless nights ten years from now? The answer is out there right now, in the brilliant work going on in bioscience labs and genetic engineering projects all around the world, driven for the most part by scientists with a totally genuine desire to improve the human condition. But in comparison to their nuclear forebears, their work is far more vulnerable to abuse, far more open to the dark side.

On 20 March 1995, the Japanese cult, Aum Shinrikyo, released nerve gas into the Tokyo subway, killing 12 people and hospitalizing more than 5000. Many saw it as a 'wake-up call' to security forces and disaster planners all around the world. Three and a half years later, in November 1998, the London *Sunday Times* regaled its readers with stories of laboratories in Indonesia and the Czech Republic openly selling mail-order *brucella*, *E-coli* and *botulinum* bugs for derisory sums of money to *Sunday Times* reporters posing as foreign scientists. It calmly informed us that MI5 had visited 700 British biotech firms, telling them they might just be targeted by countries and organizations trying to develop biological or chemical weapons. Officially, we are told, the gene recombiners haven't yet got going on these standard bio-terrorist products. But they surely will.

And on the human genetics front? You probably don't even want to think about it. Nor, in an ideal world, would I. But I was struck by an article in *New Scientist* in January 1999, highlighting the work of Craig Venter and colleagues at Celera Genomics sequencing the genomes of certain bacteria that cause human disease.

Venter's team has compared the genomes of simple micro-organisms, disrupting their genes in turn to find out which are essential for survival. They have pinpointed a minimum of 300 genes which seem to be necessary for life. In theory, they could now build an artificial chromosome carrying these genes, and wrap it up in a membrane with a few proteins and other biochemicals to create a simple synthetic organism.

This organism could reveal much about the evolution of early life on Earth. But it could also be a gift to bio-terrorists. A streamlined cell of this type would be an attractive template for building a devastating bio-weapon. 'All at once, we wondered whether we were getting into dangerous territory here,' says Venter.

Though Venter's work is extremely controversial, this is a man who's done nothing wrong. He's in breach of no regulatory system. As much as any other bio-pioneer, he's working away there for the putative benefit of humankind as well as his own company. In this particular case, he had enough natural caution voluntarily to suspend work on the project 'until the implications can be debated in full.'

Debated in full – then what? Legislate? Pointless: in a few years' time, labs capable of doing such work will be as common as labs converting South American poppies into heroin and other drugs. Individual bio-pioneers will be beyond the reach of any government. The full details of about thirty genomes are already known, with dozens more to follow in short order, with all their genetic information available from on-line databases.

As Bryan Appleyard points out in his powerful book, *Brave New Worlds*, nobody talks about this because it's just far too scary. And though scientists hate it to be said, we've simply lost control of the biosciences, and are frighteningly ill-prepared, both technically and metaphysically, to live in a world that is being systematically dismantled and then re-combined with few, if any, moral precepts to guide us. Enjoy it while you can.

Chapter 9

Science without a Soul

In September 1985, after eighteen months as Director of Friends of the Earth, I gave a talk to local groups explaining why we'd just decided to put a much higher percentage of our (then very meagre) resources into scientific research – including appointing more staff with science degrees. 'But not any old scientists', I said, 'scientists with soul and attitude is what we're after.'

A week later, one of our local Group Coordinators sent me a book by Mary Midgley called *Evolution as a Religion*. I reread it while researching this book, and enjoyed all over again her wonderfully mischievous hypothesis that even the most buttoned-down, atheistic scientists can't help lapsing into quasi-religious sentiments when let off their materialist leashes. In analysing a number of 'curiously intense purple passages that struck me as being both oddly detached from their context and also as smelling of incense and hymn books rather than the laboratory', she detected in them 'a kind of involuntary poetry, a great emotional force'.

From then on, I've been far more alert to the growing number of eloquent voices reminding us that there need be no contradiction between science and religion – let alone between science and the kind of less formulaic spiritual beliefs that for many have supplanted adherence to established religions. Science addresses itself to that which can be observed and measured, while religion and spirituality address themselves to the immeasurable – two aspects of a single reality. There need be no antagonism between them, as Professor Krishna of the Krishnamurti Foundation explains:

The scientific quest and the spiritual quest have been the two great quests of humanity. The scientific quest is to discover the order in the external world of space, time, energy and matter. The spiritual quest is to discover order in our consciousness. At their roots, both quests originated out of human inquisitiveness. We human beings want to enquire into what is happening within and around us. Since the whole of reality is built up of both matter and consciousness, why should the quest for the understanding of order in the external world be antagonistic for the quest for the understanding of order in the inner world?

('We Shall be Whole', *Resurgence*, September 1998)

The burgeoning interest in 'science and religion' as an area of legitimate academic concern is much more apparent in the United States than it seems to be in the UK. The Chicago Center for Religion and Science publishes a fascinating journal under the title of *Zygon*, and both Berkeley and Princeton have highly prestigious centres devoted to a host of cross-cutting themes. This may of course have something to do with the continuing religious commitment of most Americans – from the time pollsters first started asking about people's religious beliefs in the early 1970s, the number declaring a belief in God (or a 'universal spirit') has stayed pretty constant at around 95 per cent.

This must be a cause of continuing astonishment to whose for whom religion is at best an interesting collection of bits of cultural flotsam and jetsam beached on the shores of modern rationalism, and at worst dangerous mumbo-jumbo. Yet at the same time, the postwar model of technology-driven material progress still goes largely unquestioned by most Americans, whatever their religious affiliation may be. One of the reasons there has been so little concern about GM crops in America (in comparison to Europe) is the unthinking acceptance on their part that what the biotech companies are doing will be good for America and good for consumers. Most Americans retain an almost absolutist faith in 'progress through science'.

By contrast, the UK has far more sceptics about the prevailing model of progress, and far fewer religious fundamentalists. But we do seem to be peculiarly well provided with a supply of scientific fundamentalists engaged in an ongoing crusade to wipe out any trace of religious faith or spiritual sensibilities. Richard Dawkins (author of *The Selfish Gene* and *The Blind Watchmaker*) has taken upon himself the mantle of Crusader-in-Chief, and he regularly excoriates all fellow scientists who give way to the superstition of religion.

This particular variety of scientific fundamentalism (which some have coupled with the kind of political intolerance that underpins totalitarian regimes) is currently enjoying quite a vogue in the UK. Most of the self-styled 'popularizers' of science tend to be of this persuasion, aggressively drowning out the rather gentler tones of eminent scientists such as John Houghton (Chair of the Royal Commission on Environmental Pollution), John Polkinghorne, a particle physicist turned commentator on the role of science in society, and Ghillean Prance, until recently Director of the Royal Botanic Gardens at Kew, all of whom profess strong and articulate religious beliefs, which lend weight to rather than detract from the valuable work they do as scientists.

What is it about some scientists' religious beliefs (often encapsulated in the notion of a 'divine mind' at work behind the complex patterns of evolution) that brings out such intense hostility in other scientists? Perhaps they see themselves as the latter-day inheritors of the struggles that pitted Darwin and Thomas Huxley against the Established Church? Or is it that they see their assiduously promoted notion of science being 'value-free' shot through and through by so many scientists explicitly espousing values and belief systems that must by definition shape the work they do as scientists? Perish the thought that the Emperor of Objective Science should be seen to have no clothes precisely by comparison with the richly-clad apparel of scientists free of the illusion of value-free science.

There is one particular fallacy from which we must free ourselves, and this is the idea that contemporary scientific theories are somehow neutral, or value-free, and do not presuppose the submission of the human mind to a set of assumptions or dogmas in the way that is said to be demanded by adherence to a religious faith. Every thought, every observation, every judgment, every description, whether of the modern scientist or of anyone else, is soaked in *a priori* preconceived built-in value judgments, assumptions and dogmas at least as rigid, if not more rigid (because they are so often unconsciously embraced) than those of any explicitly religious system. The very nature of human thought is such that it cannot operate independently of value judgments, assumptions and dogmas. Even the assertion that it can constitutes a value judgment, and implies a whole philosophy whether we are aware of it or not.

Forgive me if I return to this vexed theme, through the passionate words of Philip Sherrard in *Human Image: World Image*. But it lies at the heart of my apprehension about the state of modern science, and about the capacity of modern science to be an effective force in bringing about a transition between a way of life which is already totally unsustainable for six billion people and a genuinely sustainable way of life for more than ten billion.

The problem is that the crisis we face is not in essence an ecological crisis, as Sherrard points out, but a crisis in the way we think. We treat Planet Earth in this destructive, god-forsaken way because we see things in a destructive, god-forsaken way. And we see things that way because that's how we see ourselves: as random, purposeless bipeds, with an inherently destructive nature that can be explained through our genetic inheritance; as rapacious, self-interested exploiters, whose success depends on converting all around us (other people, resources, relationships, and so on) into commodities that can be traded like so many sacks of potatoes; as victims of our own 'success' in procreational and technological terms, drawn ineluctably and still more or less uncomplainingly to the brink of ecological meltdown.

Having systematically 'desacralized' ourselves (i.e. ceased to think of ourselves as sacred beings), we've had little difficulty desacralizing the world around us, evolving a world view that strips the Earth and its creatures of any sacred significance, reducing our natural inheritance to a bank of inanimate assets uniquely available to *Homo rapiens*. This is not 'God's world' we're talking of any longer, but 'our world', subject only to our will for good or ill.

And how did this pernicious self-image arise? In large part from precisely the same model of rational, mechanistic, value-free science that started with Francis Bacon, and to which we are now invited to turn yet again in order to find a way out of the evolutionary cul-de-sac in which we're stuck. Yet if we used just a little of that inductive logic of which scientists are so fond, tracking the symptoms of today's environmental crisis back to the way we see ourselves, via the way we see the world, then is it not reasonable to hypothesize that we are unlikely to be able to sort out those symptoms in any lasting way unless we first sort out the way we see the world – which in turn means a revolution in the way we see ourselves.

For me, that's where the cold, intolerant reductionism of Richard Dawkins and Lewis Wolpert becomes politically lethal. In rejecting out-of-hand both the indigenous wisdom and the contemporary yearning of people for whom every part of the Earth (and of the whole Cosmos) remains sacred, they deprive us of precisely the kind of crucial moral, ethical and emotional resources without which the transition to a sustainable world looks all but impossible.

The Gaia Debate

That's what makes the continuing debate about the value of the 'Gaia hypothesis' so significant. Back in 1979, Jim Lovelock (for me the UK's most eminent and inspiring independent scientist) published *Gaia: a New Look at Life on Earth*. For twenty years, it has continued to stir controversy and delight in equal measure, with both Lovelock and US microbiologist Lynn Margulis (with whom he initially developed the Gaia hypothesis) publishing subsequent works that have greatly enhanced our understanding of the ways of the world and evolution.

The Gaia hypothesis suggests that the Earth's climate and surface environment are in some degree regulated by the totality of plants, animals and micro-organisms that make up life. It suggests that the Earth is not some inanimate lump of rock on which life has evolved purely by random chance, but rather 'a biological super-organism' that modifies and regulates itself, acting like a planetary thermostatic control system. Just as all mammals are able to maintain astonishingly stable internal temperatures despite dramatic changes in external temperature, so the Earth keeps both its surface temperature and the composition of gases in the atmosphere stable.

Whole shelves in libraries are now filled with books about Gaia, and it's clearly not possible to go into too much detail in a short work of this kind. But two 'Gaia issues' are particularly interesting in terms of the insights they offer us about science today and the differences between scientists like Richard Dawkins and Jim Lovelock.

Firstly, when discussing the notion of the Earth as a self-regulating organism, there are all sorts of different ways of defining what we mean by 'regulation'. As the debate has evolved, four distinct positions have emerged: that the interaction of all the millions of different species that constitute life on Earth inevitably influences the global environment as they 'co-evolve' – which it's hard to disagree with, and something that even Richard Dawkins could sign up to; that life actually modifies the global environment – which is usually adopted as the compromise position; that life positively regulates the global environment – as Lovelock once said, 'living organisms must regulate their environment in order to survive'; and finally, that life not only regulates the environment, but does so purposefully, and with intent.

You can precisely determine the orthodoxy of scientists' opinions by getting them to place themselves on that continuum. The most rigorous neo-Darwinians abhor the notion of life regulating the global environment, and become apoplectic at the mere suggestion that this is happening purposefully. They reject out of hand the idea of a unified planetary system that in some way overarches the countless evolutionary shifts in individual species brought about through random natural selection. How could Gaia possibly 'cool her entire body' to compensate for increasing heat from the sun? How is it possible that life writ large could be optimizing conditions for its own uses? How could life plan, let alone execute, any such design? As many have pointed out, the passion with which they attack such 'biological heresies' has all the hallmarks of the adherents of a religious faith, which is of course what Darwinism has become for many scientists today.

By contrast, interdisciplinary system-thinkers and proponents of a more holistic emphasis on the relationships between individual organisms, rather than exclusively focusing on individual organisms in their own right, are relaxed about the idea of a self-regulating planet – though it has to be said that there are few takers for the notion of purposeful self-regulation!

Lovelock's own position on the continuum has been a matter of great interest. In the original 1979 work, he came down more at the intentionality end of the continuum, suggesting, for instance, that as a living super-organism, Gaia not only regulated the combination of gases in the atmosphere that made life on Earth possible, but had to be doing so intentionally. As he put it then: 'The biosphere has assumed the capacity for planetary control.'

This ensured a terrible hammering at the hands of the ever-vigilant neo-Darwinians, and since then he seems to have moved somewhat to the middle of the spectrum, confessing to the sin of 'teleological fallacy' (by attributing purposefulness where no purpose could possibly exist), without ever giving up his commitment to a 'strong Gaia'. His latest articulation of this was made in a speech to the Gaia Society in July 1999:

> When life began, over 3.5 billion years ago, organisms used the planet's raw materials and returned their wastes and dead bodies. Doing this changed the chemical composition of the atmosphere, ocean and surface rock. Evolution by natural selection ensured that those organisms which change their environment so as to favour their progeny flourished, while those who poisoned or made it barren, died out. From this convergent evolution of life and the Earth emerged Gaia, our comfortable, self-regulating planet.

Lovelock had originally settled on the name of the Greek goddess Gaia as a title on the recommendation of his friend, the novelist William Golding. But he was gradually persuaded that scientists would never take the idea seriously without a less intellectually suspect name. 'Global geophysiology' was advanced as the best alternative. In an entertaining article in *New Scientist* in 1994, leading science journalist Fred Pearce exhorted Lovelock to stay true to Gaia:

Is Lovelock trying to secure Gaia's place in orthodoxy to make peace with the scientific community that once came close to disowning him altogether? Does the heretic suddenly fear the flames of academic oblivion? He says that 'the acceptance of geophysiology in science will be delayed if those who should know better continue to talk about the Gaia hypothesis'. But is this not an appalling indictment of scientists, implying that they are unable to cope with heresies, and are forever papering over the cracks in reductionist thought? Gaia as metaphor; Gaia as a catalyst for scientific enquiry; Gaia as literal truth; Gaia as Earth Goddess: whoever she is, let's keep her. If science cannot find room for the grand vision, if Gaia dare not speak her name in *Nature*, then shame on science. To recant now would be a terrible thing, Jim. Don't do it.

But he nearly did. Only after years of wrangling was Gaia: the Society for Research and Education in Earth System Science formally launched in 1998, appropriately enough at the Royal Society itself, that bastion of scientific orthodoxy. Gaia and geophysiology now co-exist in an uneasy titular symbiosis, an intriguing reflection on the second issue I want to touch on: Gaia as science and Gaia as religion. This has dogged Lovelock and Margulis right from the start, with the Gaia hypothesis liberating as much spiritual energy as scientific energy.

Back in 1986, Lynn Margulis declared 'the religious overtones of Gaia make me sick', and compared the 'New Age distortions' of Gaian theory to the distortion of the science of genetics into eugenics. In her book *The Symbiotic Planet* (1998), the final chapter of which provides a splendidly trenchant and authoritative synopsis of the power of the Gaia idea, she is still castigating those who personify Gaia as 'a nurturing Mother Earth, a living goddess who will supposedly punish or reward us for our environmental insults or blessings to her body.' This hangover from Greek mythology is deeply offensive: 'Gaia is neither vicious nor nurturing in relation to humanity; it is a convenient name for an Earth-wide phenomenon: temperature, acidity/alkalinity, and gas composition regulation. Gaia is a series of interacting ecosystems that compose a single huge ecosystem at the Earth's surface. Period.'

Her contempt for any spiritual interpretation of Gaia is not so much an expression of intolerant atheism as of her despair at the limitless capacity of humankind to delude itself as to its special evolutionary role:

> Gaia is an ancient phenomenon. Trillions of jostling, feeding, mating, exuding beings compose her planetary system. Gaia, a tough bitch, is not at all threatened by humans. Planetary life survived at least three billion years before humanity was even the dream of a lively ape with a yearning for a hairless mate. Humans are not the centre of life, nor is any other single species. Humans are not even central to life. We are a recent, rapidly-growing part of an enormous ancient whole.

Lovelock himself has always been much more relaxed about the spiritual aspect of Gaia ('at least Gaia may turn out to be the first religion to have a testable scientific theory embedded in it'). At the very least, Gaian thinking offers a powerful secular alternative to the kind of dominant humanism that continues to put the human species at the very apex of life on earth, contrary to all scientific evidence about evolution. Beyond that, the four-billion-year evolution of Gaia provides us with a 'cosmic story' which can be embraced by people of all cultures and all religions, and could play a central role in helping us to redefine our view of ourselves and our view of the world.

Wholeness

So what's the problem? For Gaia to thrive in two intellectual domains should surely be seen as a tribute to the power of the idea rather than a source of crabby scientific embarrassment? (Incidentally, I've never heard any spiritually-minded Gaians inveighing against the mean-minded reductionist scientists expropriating their goddess!) Many Christians and followers of other world faiths have seen the power inherent in this unifying symbol. The Reverend James Morton, Dean of the Cathedral of St John the Divine in New York City, puts it as follows (as quoted in Joseph Lawrence's 1990 book, *Gaia: The Growth of an Idea*):

The living earth principle gives us strong images and metaphors that require an inclusive way of understanding, a religious way of comprehending the greater whole. After all, the word 'religion' does mean, at its roots, to knit together. Not at all unlike the Gaian idea of global interdependence, environment and organisms knit together as one. In this way, Gaia may prove less a set of specific beliefs than a way to reincorporate faith into daily life.

But for scientists who find all this 'eco-la-la' (as Murray Bookchin once famously dismissed the spiritual dimension of environmentalism) either perturbing or deeply embarrassing, is the concept of Gaia any the less astonishing and inspiring if stripped of its spiritual overlay? I think not. The idea of the world as a seamless whole in which all parts are constantly and intimately interacting with each other is both humbling and uplifting. In an unpublished article of 1996, the philosopher Ervin Laszlo has speculated about the long-term impacts this could have on our view of ourselves and the world, as we shift from thinking about planet Earth 'as a lifeless rock to a whispering pond'.

How we relate to each other and to nature depends on our concepts of nature, of life, and of the human being. If we believe that nature is a lifeless mechanism, a collection of passive rocks, we will come to believe that we are entitled to do with it as we please, so long as we do not act against our own interests. If we look on animals and other people as but more complex machines, we shall manipulate them too. We will cut out their disfunctioning parts and organs, splice up their genes, or re-wire the circuitries of their brain. But what if nature is not a passive rock or a lifeless machine? What if people are not just more complex machines, and are not separate from each other and from the environment, but profoundly though subtly linked? And what if the entire cosmos throbs with the creative energy of self-organization, constantly evolving, with periodic bursts of explosive innovation? If this is the concept we get from science, would we still relate to each other and to our environment in quite the same way?

Does this portend a 'new religion', as some (including Richard Dawkins) have argued? That seems far too grand a notion for what is in effect no more than a re-orientation, both physical and metaphysical: instead of the 'ontological assumption of separateness', which has driven Western models of progress and science since the time of Francis Bacon, should we not restructure those models of progress and science (in Willis Harman's words) 'on an ontological assumption of oneness and wholeness'?

It's an impertinence, for a non-scientist, but I have come to believe that such an orientation would prove immensely helpful to scientists trying to find a more effective way of engaging in the kind of issues explored in this book. The pernicious illusion of value-free science seems to have given a large number of scientists a licence to disengage from the interlocking crises we now find ourselves in the midst of. In my twenty-five years as an environmental activist, I've met literally hundreds of scientists who have become adept at suppressing their own values and passions out of an implicit or explicit fear of their work being corrupted by such suspect tendencies.

A deeper understanding of the utter impossibility of either physical or psychic disconnection from the rest of life in Earth might just provide a twenty-first-century licence to engage in the thick of things, instead of just looking on from afar. A licence to engage as citizen-scientists, as alert to the social and ethical importance of the work they're doing as they are to its intellectual and technical significance. Why be afraid of that 'great emotional force'?

Chapter 10

Two Cultures: One World

Still rumbling along behind every debate about the role of modern science is C.P. Snow's theory of 'two cultures' – the arts and the sciences – with the gap between the two widening all the time as each and every branch of science becomes increasingly specialized and esoteric. Clichéd though it rapidly became, I was always very taken with the 'two cultures' thesis, especially as I struggled to narrow my own personal knowledge gap in the Green Party and Friends of the Earth. Since then, however, I've become more and more disenchanted with its ritual incantation by the COPUS crowd, and have come to see it as a secondary and not particularly relevant reflection on the role of science today.

Far more problematic and far more divisive is the gap between those people (scientists and non-scientists alike) whose lives are still geared to a philosophy and practice that sets the human race apart from the rest of life on Earth, weighed down as they are by the ontological assumption of separateness, and those people (scientists and non-scientists alike) who see the world for the unified system it really is, buoyed up by the ontological assumption of oneness. Narrowing that gap is infinitely more important than narrowing the gap between scientists and non-scientists. Without progress on this score, the entire environmental cause (which seems at last to be making some progress) may yet founder.

There is no challenge more pressing nor more fundamental than developing a genuinely sustainable way of life for humankind. All else is secondary. If we cannot secure the biophysical foundations on which our lives depend, then every other challenge we face (be it spiritual, political or economic) will by definition become entirely irrelevant.

Despite the much higher levels of environmental awareness in the late 1990s, this assertion would still be contested by a large majority of politically active people. Many continue to subscribe to what the World Business Council for Sustainable Development describes as the FROG (First Raise Our Growth) mentality: we must go on getting richer so that we will eventually have enough money to sort out all the environmental problems caused during the process of getting rich. Many more would put the pursuit of social justice first, on the grounds that only when societies are more equal will people feel inclined to address their environmental problems. And most of them haven't even begun to wrap their minds around the meaning and implications of sustainability at all. Regrettable though it may be, there is as yet no sufficiently compelling reason for politicians to confront the inherently unsustainable nature of industrial capitalism.

So where does that leave the use of science in environmental policy-making? As Robin Grove-White says, 'The fundamental point remains, that at the level of policy, particular constructions of "science" have been harnessed routinely to the service of whatever the dominant official priorities of the day have happened to be.' Given that science is always framed, and even directed, by prevailing political and economic realities (whatever the die-hard proponents of value-free science may continue to argue), no one should be too surprised that the contribution it is currently making to that sustainability challenge is equally inadequate.

This inadequacy manifests itself at many different levels, the most profound of which touches on that hoary old issue of 'the meaning of life'. From Francis Bacon onwards, we have been progressively seduced into a state of mind that asserts that there is no meaning beyond that which can be observed and measured, and that we humans are nothing more than random organisms making a pretty messy job of our short span of life on Earth.

As Philip Sherrard points out in *Human Image: World Image*, there's something terminally self-defeating in this denial of a deeper meaning or purpose:

Every extension of the empire and influence of our contemporary secular scientific mentality has gone hand in hand with a corresponding and increased erosion in us of the sense of the sacred. In fact, we do not have any respect, let alone reverence, for the world of nature because we do not fundamentally have any respect, let alone reverence, for ourselves. It is because we've lost the sense of our own reality that we've lost the sense of every other reality as well. It is because we cripple and mutilate ourselves that we cripple and mutilate everything else as well. Our contemporary crisis is really our own depravity writ large.

We have, of course, been here many times before. In the nineteenth century, the Romantic poets battled against the overbearing 'philosophy' of the Enlightenment, rejecting outright the notion that Newton's laws could be held to obtain in every corner of human life, and that all else should yield to reason and logic. In his poem, *Lamia*, Keats warned:

> Philosophy will clip an Angel's wings,
> Conquer all mysteries by rule and line,
> Empty the haunted air, and gnomed mine –
> Unweave a rainbow.

In this respect, science is still of little use in retrieving what has been described as 'our essential humanity'. The idea that science can provide the answer to everything, in one great unified theory, should be seen for the absurd arrogance it really is. Even in its own materialist, reductionist terms, the answers that science comes up with are often flawed and little more than the catalyst for the next generation of problems to which yet more flawed answers must be found. As Fritz Schumacher put it in his *Guide for the Perplexed* (1977): 'The maps produced by modern materialistic scientism leave all the questions that really matter unanswered. More than that, they do not even show a way to a possible answer: they deny the validity of the questions.'

Beyond that, I suggested in Chapter 2 that there were six directional shifts that will need to be speeded up if science is to play a more purposeful and less ambivalent role in helping to deliver a sustainable future. Looking at those six shifts, what conclusions can we draw about the state of science in the environment today?

1   Science will need to become more precautionary.
Progress report: Fair to good.
The Precautionary Principle is now in play (as long as absolutist interpretations of it do not render it useless as a policy tool), and reasonably hard at work in processes like the Intergovernmental Panel on Climate Change. Even when they do not come to it naturally, as it were, politicians and businesspeople may well be forced into more precautionary approaches as their electors and consumers withdraw the confidence they once took for granted. Responsible and precautionary practices are likely to become an even more essential element in the pursuit of 'a licence to operate' in modern society.

2   Science will need to become more participative.
Progress Report: Fair only.
As we've seen, we've only scratched the surface of what has been described as 'civic science' in the UK, not least because of the reluctance of a very large number of scientists to get stuck into all such processes. But the Royal Commission's 1998 Report is undoubtedly a landmark in promoting such processes, which are, by any standard, right up New Labour's street anyway.

3   Scientists will need to become less arrogant.
Progress Report: Poor.
But whose fault is that? We've made such gods of our scientists in modern times, looking up to them more or less unquestioningly as dispensers of authority, knowledge and new technology (if not of wisdom), that more than a little arrogance was to be expected. Optimists argue that scientists have now been pushed off their pedestal and will be the better for it; pessimists detect little change in the way so many of them talk down to people from one culture (the only true culture, as it were) to another (not really culture at all). And for all their

strictures about public ignorance and superstition (especially when they're put on the spot in any particular environmental controversy), it seems to me that most people have developed an intuitively sharp if still inconsistent understanding of the strengths and weaknesses of modern science.

4 Science will need to be more independent and more transparent.
Progress Report: Poor.
He who pays the piper calls the tune. The almost total dependence of most universities in America (and increasingly in Europe) on research grants from the private sector has severely eroded the level of confidence that many people have in the quality of scientists' work. In many industries, secrecy is still endemic, and not just for reasons of commercial confidentiality. Governments are at least bound by a range of 'freedom of information' constraints, but the rearguard action being fought by Home Secretary Jack Straw to deny UK citizens access to research findings which their money has paid for, demonstrates both the conservatism of this particular government and the desperate lengths that most politicians will go to to continue operating behind closed doors.

5 Scientists will need to become more compassionate.
Progress Report: Uncertain.
This is not a quality that lends itself easily to measurement. Generalizations are usually offensive, and not very helpful. Science is a two-edged sword: in the hands of some, it is wielded as the sword of truth, compassion and visionary humanitarianism; in the hands of others, it becomes a weapon of oppression, abuse and the wholesale exploitation of people and planet alike.

6 Science will need to become more holistic.
Progress Report: Fair to good.
Inspired by E.O. Wilson's book *Consilience* (1999), in which he argues passionately for the unification of knowledge and different scientific disciplines, and still invigorated (twenty years on) by the sweep and

ambition of the Gaia hypothesis, I'd argue this is one area where things may well change much faster than currently seems possible. Narrow reductionism seems such a waste of our full cerebral potential, and may be judged in history as nothing more than a serious but temporary failure of our entire educational system.

At a deeper level, however, the speed at which an ontological assumption of oneness will take over from the prevailing ontological assumption of separateness is another matter. That may well take some further shock to the human system, some traumatic reminder of the elemental indivisibility and interconnectedness of all living things. The steady accretion of hard evidence to that effect over the last few decades has as yet proved insufficient to dismantle the philosophical illusion that has shaped our lives for so many hundreds of years.

This book started with the question: is modern science in a fit state – philosophically and methodologically – to enable us to meet the challenge of sustainability? The answer must be 'no'. Not 'no' for ever; there is no reason why a more enlightened understanding of 'sound science' should not underpin the transition to a sustainable society as effectively and helpfully as 'sound science' today underpins industrial capitalism. But 'no' for now.

Which leaves me well and truly mired in the same ambivalence with which I started: we can't do without modern science, and surely wouldn't want to; yet we can't do what we want to do – and need to do – with it. So how fast a transition can we look forward to?

I was putting the finishing touches to the main text of this book precisely at the time of the thirtieth anniversary of the Apollo moonflight. Those shots of the Earth taken from the Apollo spacecraft didn't exactly change my life then and there in August 1969, but undoubtedly helped shape my early environmental interests. Not so much because I started thinking of the Earth as 'fragile', as so many contemporary commentators seemed to do, but because of the wholeness of what I saw. The Earth, as one system, all of a piece, not broken down into continents, countries, poles, weather zones, ecosystems, and so on.

Over the years, this has clearly had a huge impact on many people. The early literature of that wave of new NGOs set up in the 1970s (including Friends of the Earth and Greenpeace) was heavily influenced by those images; Jim Lovelock acknowledged their power in framing his Gaia hypothesis in the late 1970s; and in 1987, the Brundtland Report articulated that perception-changing influence:

> In the middle of the twentieth century, we saw our planet from space for the first time. Historians may eventually find that this vision had a greater impact on thought than did the Copernican revolution of the sixteenth century, which upset humans' self-image by revealing that the Earth is not the centre of the universe. From space, we see a small and fragile ball dominated not by human activity and edifice, but by a pattern of clouds, oceans, greenery and soils. Humanity's inability to fit its activities into that pattern is changing planetary systems fundamentally.

Since then, many more commentators have talked of this moment as ushering in one of those great discontinuities that mark the intellectual development of the human species, akin to the Darwinian revolution, which displaced the human species from its self-assumed position at the apex of creation.

Writing in the May 1999 issue of *Environmental Values*, Sheila Jasanoff explores the significance of that unique historical moment – 'a moment defined by such radically new ways of seeing the Earth that science was forced, in effect, to adopt a new environmental paradigm.' A paradigm which stresses the interconnectedness of all living and non-living systems; a paradigm premised on the ontological assumption of oneness. But how much further does this really take us? Are we, as environmentalist Lynton Caldwell suggests, 'temporary resident custodians', or in the words of Lynn Margulis, 'upright mammalian weeds'. As Jasanoff points out:

> These two views of humankind – interloper versus custodian – clearly imply very different moral obligations in relation to the biosphere. The

scientific theory of ecological interconnectedness leaves unanswered some fundamental questions about what human beings are entitled to do with their environment. This is because the ecological paradigm focuses on the physical constraints of the biosphere without paying much attention to the economic, aesthetic, moral or spiritual dimensions of our relationship to the world around us.

Here too, one suspects, science can't really help. Biologically speaking, we are both interloper and custodian; spiritually speaking, we can see ourselves as either, but there is a world of difference. To reconcile ourselves to the role of interloper, indifferently working out our allotted evolutionary span like any other transient species, seems so despairingly unhuman. There must be something between such a cowardly cosmological cop-out, and those fantasies of evolutionary pre-eminence and control so devastatingly lampooned by Lynn Margulis:

> To me, the human move to take responsibility for the living Earth is laughable – the rhetoric of the powerless. The planet takes care of us, not we of it. Our self-inflated moral imperative to guide a wayward Earth or heal our sick planet is evidence of our immense capacity for self-delusion. Rather, we need to protect us from ourselves.

It is precisely that need to protect ourselves that lends the role of steward or custodian both dignity and lasting meaning. For a secular humanist, it provides incentive enough to break through the paradigm of separateness and redefine human purpose within an ethos of stewardship. For those of a more religious or spiritual orientation, our principal purpose must be to recover a sense of our true identity as sacred beings. Philip Sherrard again:

> Once we repossess a sense of our own holiness, we will recover the sense of the holiness of the world about us as well, and we will then act towards the world about us with the awe and humility that we should possess when we enter a sacred shrine, a temple of love and beauty in which we

worship and adore. Only in this way will we once again become aware that our destiny and the destiny of nature are one and the same. Only in this way can we restore a cosmic harmony.

'Cosmic harmony' and discussions about the role of science in the modern world are extremely infrequent bedfellows. Apart from the writings of the likes of Stephen Hawking (whose work remains incomprehensible to the vast majority of people), and one or two serious popularizers like Melvyn Bragg (the British novelist and arts supremo who has laboured mightily and very effectively to make science past and present much more accessible to non-scientists), there's very little reflective thought in contemporary scientific enterprise. Its onward rush gathers all before it, with politicians, commentators and citizens watching from the sidelines with a mixture of wonder and deep apprehension.

It's not easy to reconcile that exuberant, devil-take-the-hindmost spirit with the quest for a genuinely sustainable and more equitable future. For many of today's pioneers, pushing endlessly on into new territory, safety first, the precautionary principle, and 'due diligence' all look like so many constraining shackles, purpose-built to hold them back and diminish the contribution they feel they have to make to the advancement of the human species. But constrain them we must, intelligently and purposefully, if that prospect of a sustainable future is to become a reality.

Appleyard, Brian, *Understanding the Present: Science and the Soul of Modern Man*, London, 1992

Attiyah, Michael, 'Science Must Recover the Moral High Ground', based on final address as President of the Royal Society, 30 November, *Financial Times*, London, 19 December 1995

Bacon, Francis, *Temporus Partus Masculus* (The Masculine Birth of Time), London, 1612

Beck, Ulrich, and Mark Ritter, *Risk Society: Towards a New Modernity*, London, 1992

Caldwell, Lynton, *International Environment Policy: Emergence and Dimensions*, Durham, N. Carolina, 1984

Callenbach, Ernest, *Ecotopia: A Novel About Ecology, People and Politics in 1999*, Berkeley, Calif., 1975; London, 1978

Carson, Rachel, *Silent Spring*, Cambridge, Mass., 1962; London, 1963

Colborn, Theo, Dianne Dumanoski and John Peterson Myers, *Our Stolen Future: A Scientific Detective Story*, London and New York, 1996

The Cornerhouse, *Briefing Number 10: Genetic Engineering and World Hunger*, Sturminster Newton, Dorset, October 1998

Ehrlich, Paul, *The Machinery of Nature*, New York, 1986; London, 1988

Fagin, Dan, and Marianne Lavelle, *Toxic Deception: How the Chemical Industry Manipulates Science, Bends the Law and Endangers Your Health*, Secaucus, N. J., 1996

Freedland, Jonathan, 'Goodbye to the Oracle', *Guardian*, London, 9 June 1999

Gerard, Simon, *New Scientist*, London, 21 February 1998

Greenfield, Susan, 'When Shall We Three Meet Again?', ('Under the Microscope' series), *Review, Independent on Sunday*, London, 2 November 1997

Grove-White, Robin, 'On "Sound Science", the Environment and Political Authority', *Environmental Values*, Vol. 8, No. 2, Isle of Harris, May 1999

—, 'Environment, Risk and Democracy', *Greening the Millennium, The Political Quarterly*, Oxford, 1997

Hall, Ross Hume, 'The Medical-Industrial Complex', *Ecologist*, Vol. 28, No. 2, Sturminster Newton, Dorset, March–April 1998

Hawken, Paul, 'The Natural Step, US Founding Brochure', San Francisco, 1996

Ho, Mae-Wan, *Genetic Engineering: Dream or Nightmare? The Brave New World of Bad Science and Big Business*, Bath, 1998

Jackson, Tim, *Material Concerns: Pollution, Profit and Quality of Life*, London, 1996

Jasanoff, Sheila, 'The Songlines of Risk', *Environmental Values*, Vol. 8, No. 2, Isle of Harris, May 1999

Krishna, P., 'We Shall Be Whole', *Resurgence*, Issue 190, Hartland, Devon, September 1998

Laszlo, Ervin, 'The Emerging Vision of Science', unpublished article, 1992

Lawrence, Joseph, *Gaia: The Growth of an Idea*, London and New York, 1990

Levinson, Ralph, 'Let's Sup Awhile', *New Scientist*, London, 13 February 1999

Lovelock, James, *Gaia: A New Look at Life on Earth*, New York and Oxford, 1979

—, speech to the Gaia Society, quoted *Guardian*, London, 4 August 1999

Margulis, Lynn, *The Symbiotic Planet: A New Look at Evolution*, London, 1998

Midgley, Mary, *Evolution as a Religion*, London and New York, 1985

—, *True to this Earth*, Oxford, 1995

O'Riordan, Tim, *Environmental Science for Environmental Management*, New York, 1995; London, 1999

Pearce, Fred, 'Gaia, Gaia, Don't Go Away', *New Scientist*, London, 28 May 1994

Rifkin, Jeremy, *The Biotech Century: Harnessing the Gene and Remaking the World*, London and New York, 1998

Roszak, Theodore, *The Memoirs of Elizabeth Frankenstein*, New York, 1995; London, 1996

—, *The Voice of the Earth: An Exploration of Eco Psychology*, New York, 1982; London, 1993

The Royal Society, *GM Plants for Food Use*, London, September 1998

Schumacher, E.F., *A Guide for the Perplexed*, London and New York, 1977

—, *Small is Beautiful: A Study of Economics as if People Mattered*, London, 1973; New York, 1974

Shelley, Mary, *Frankenstein*, first published London, 1818

Shepherd, Linda Jean, *Lifting the Veil: the Feminine Face of Science*, Boston, Mass., 1993

Sherrard, Philip, *Human Image: World Image*, Ipswich, 1992

Skakkebaek, Niels, et al., 'Evidence for Decreasing Quality of Semen During the Past Fifty Years', *British Medical Journal*, Vol. 305, No. 12, London, September 1992

—, and Richard Sharpe, 'Are Oestrogens Involved in Falling Sperm Counts and Disorders of the Male Reproductive Tract?' *The Lancet*, London, 29 May 1993

Slater, David, 'Sound Science and the Public Perception of Risk', paper to Environment Agency Board, September 1997

Steingraber, Sandra, *Living Downstream: An Ecologist Looks at Cancer and the Environment*, New York, 1997; London, 1998

Suzuki, David, and Amanda McConnell, *The Sacred Balance: Rediscovering our Place in Nature*, London, 1999

Union of Concerned Scientists, *World Scientists' Warning to Humanity*, Cambridge, Mass., November 1992

Wilson, Edward O., *Biophilia*, Cambridge, Mass., 1984

—, and Wilson, Edmund O., *Consilience*, New York, 1999

Winston, Mark, *Nature Wars: People vs Pests*, Cambridge, Mass., and London, 1997

Worcester, Robert M., speech to the Foundation for Science and Technology, London, 12 July 1999

World Commission on Environment and Development, *Our Common Future*, Oxford, 1987

Youngson, Robert, *Scientific Blunders*, London, 1998

INDEX

DATE DUE